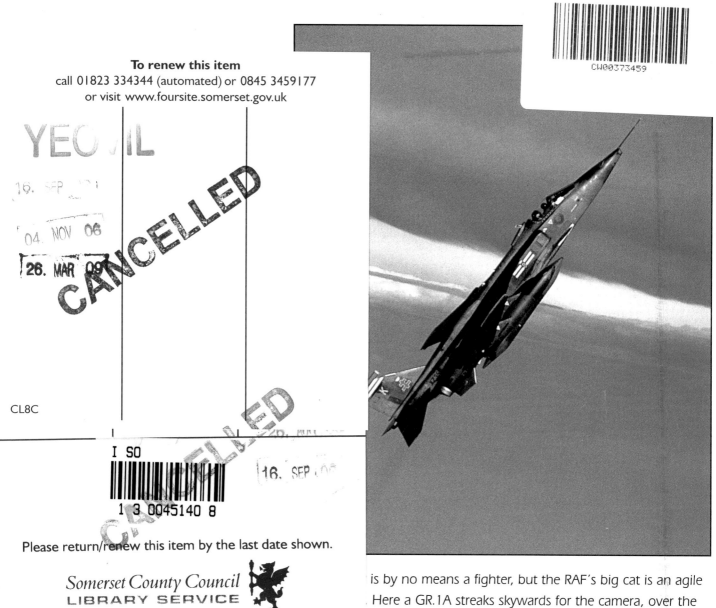

is by no means a fighter, but the RAF's big cat is an agile
. Here a GR.1A streaks skywards for the camera, over the
North Sea.

Cover illustrations

Main image: A Tornado F.3 streaks skywards. **Right:** Streaking over a
former Vulcan dispersal, the Red Arrows go through their paces during
a display rehearsal at Scampton. **Bottom left:** The venerable Wessex
completed its long career as an SAR helicopter in 1997, when the last
examples were withdrawn. The RAF's SAR fleet is now entirely
composed of Sea Kings. **Bottom right:** A head-on view of the
magnificent Phantom emphasises the huge Spey engine intakes and
the distinctive upturned wingtips.

A pair of No. 1435 Flight Tornado F.3s over the Falkland Islands. The Maltese cross emblem on the tail denotes the fact that the unit was assigned to the defence of Malta during the Second World War.

Your Royal Air Force

Ready And Focused

TIM LAMING

CASSELL PLC

ARMS AND ARMOUR

The view from the Hercules cabin's astrodome as a C.1P takes on fuel from a C.1K tanker. Although the C.1Ks are now retired, the new C-130Js soon to enter RAF service will all be tanker-capable, and part of the new Hercules fleet is almost certain to be converted to a dual tanker/transport role.

Contents

Arms & Armour Press
An Imprint of the Cassell Group
Wellington House, 125 Strand, London WC2R 0BB

Distributed in the USA by Sterling Publishing Co. Inc., 387 Park Avenue South, New York, NY 10016-8810.

British Library Cataloguing-in-Publication Data: a catalogue record for this book is available from the British Library

ISBN 1-85409-440-8

Designed and edited by DAG Publications Ltd. Designed by David Gibbons; layout by Anthony A. Evans; edited by Philip Jarrett; printed and bound in Italy.

Introduction

The 80th anniversary of the formation of the Royal Air Force falls on 1 April 1998, and this book celebrates the RAF's birthday through a series of colour images which illustrate the Service's operations over the past few years. Accompanying the text is an account of the RAF's current equipment, and a more detailed look at some of its operations, giving the reader an exciting taste of what it is like to fly and fight with today's RAF.

Below: An intimate in-flight view of a No. 74 Squadron Phantom pilot, high over Suffolk.

A book of this nature is always a challenge to produce, and the most difficult task was that of deciding which images should be included and which, because of space limitations, should be left out. Certainly, the emphasis of this book is on the more recent years of the RAF's history, as there would be little point in exploring the First and Second World War eras given the extremely limited amount of colour photographic material available. On the other hand, a book which looked just at the present day would preclude the possibility of illustrating some of the most outstanding aircraft types to have served with the RAF. Consequently, the resulting selection of images combines the new and 'not so new', and hopefully provides an interesting mix which reflects the diverse and fascinating nature of the RAF's operations.

Having taken virtually all of these pictures myself, I am obliged to thank the countless individuals within the RAF who have given so freely of their time to arrange visits, clear paperwork and even to fly me on occasions. I could not even begin to list everyone who deserves acknowledgement, but, to use a cliché, you know who you are, and I am extremely grateful for your efforts. However, my illustrious colleague John Hale deserves a special thank you for his contributions. I hope this book will serve as some small tribute to the men and women of the RAF in this, the Service's 80th year. Happy Birthday!

Tim Laming

Valedictory

Right: The BBMF remains ever-popular, its Spitfires, Hurricanes and Lancaster giving pleasure to thousands of spectators every year.

Right: Wearing representative prototype markings, Spitfire PR.XIX PS915 was one of the last Spitfires to serve operationally with the RAF.

Right: The BBMF's much-loved Avro Lancaster, PA474, better known as City of Lincoln.

Above: The Gloster Meteor (top) and de Havilland Vampire were the RAF's advanced jet trainers during the 1950s. This nationally famous duo made numerous air show appearances until they were both lost in a flying accident.

Below: The RAF's first operational jet fighter, the Gloster Meteor has long since disappeared from service. However, one Meteor remains active with the DRA at Llanbedr, acting as an airborne shepherd for unmanned drones used for RAF missile firing practice.

Above: One of the most famous aircraft ever to serve with the RAF, the Hawker Hunter was for many years the mainstay of RAF Fighter Command. It later saw service as an outstanding ground-attack aircraft, and a handful remained active into the 1990s, as illustrated, serving as conversion/continuation trainers for the RAF's Buccaneer squadrons (there being no dual-control version of the Buccaneer).

Below: Another classic aircraft which served with the RAF for many years was the Douglas Dakota. This former RAF example flew with the RAE/DRA for many years on transport duties and was then transferred back to RAF command to join the BBMF.

Left: After joining the BBMF, the former DRA Dakota was repainted in more traditional but less attractive camouflage colours, enabling the aircraft to appear as a display item in its own right as well as performing transport duties for the Flight.

Left: The venerable Avro Shackleton is perhaps the most famous of the RAF's maritime aircraft. Standing guard at RAF St Mawgan, this ex-airborne early warning (AEW) radar platform has been restored to its original ASW configuration.

Left: Although the 'Shack' served in the AEW role as a stop-gap measure, extensive delays and the eventual cancellation of the Nimrod AEW programme led to the type being retained in RAF service for many years.

Right: A Shackleton AEW.2 of No. 8 Squadron flies high above No. 12 Squadron's HAS complex at Lossiemouth. Before it was replaced by the Boeing Sentry AWACS aircraft, the Shackleton provided the RAF with a distinctly old-technology AEW capability.

Right: The Hawker Siddeley Andover was operated as both a communications and transport aircraft by the RAF, the former version equipping the Queen's Flight for many years.

Left and centre left: The transport derivative of the Andover featured a distinctive upturned rear fuselage incorporating a rear-loading cargo door. A handful of aircraft were converted to E.3 standard for radar and radio calibration duties, as illustrated by this example from No. 115 Squadron.

Left: Only two Andovers remain in service, one (illustrated) belonging to the Empire Test Pilots School and another assigned to the 'Open Skies' East-West monitoring programme.

Above: The awesome sight of an English Electric Lightning, the last all-British fighter, low over the North Sea. The Lightning's RAF career ended in 1988.

Below: Wearing the markings of No. 11 Squadron, this particular Lightning now resides with the Yorkshire Air Museum at Elvington.

Left: The portly fuselage of the two-seat Lightning T.5 is depicted in this nostalgic view of RAF Binbrook, complete with the control tower which was demolished shortly after the base was closed.

Above: A close-up of a Lightning F.6, showing the empty port missile rail and the distinctive bolt-on refuelling probe.

Right: A Lightning T.5 and an F.6 together over the North Sea. The RAF will resume single-seat fighter operations with the arrival of the Eurofighter at the turn of the century.

Right: After completing a distinguished RAF career, a small number of Lightnings were assigned to the Tornado F.3 radar development programme, flying from Warton as high-speed targets.

Top left: The RAF's last flying Vulcan, XH558, touches down at Waddington.

Centre left: Perhaps the most famous (and certainly the most recognisable) post-war RAF aircraft, the Avro Vulcan served in the strategic strike/attack role until replaced by the Tornado GR.1. From 1982 a small number of Vulcans were operated as single-point refuelling tankers, illustrated by this example from No. 50 Squadron.

Left: Retained for air display appearances, XH558 was the first Vulcan B.2 to be delivered to the RAF. Initially operating in the strike role, it was modified for maritime radar reconnaissance operations and finally to tanker configuration.

Above: Hugely popular with the public, the Vulcan's appearances at air shows ended when XH558's overhaul bill became too large for the Ministry of Defence. The aircraft was sold to a civilian buyer and currently awaits Civil Aviation Authority permission to fly again.

Left: The magnificent Buccaneer has finally retired, its role having been assumed by Tornado GR.1Bs. Initially unwanted by the RAF, as it was regarded as a distinctly naval aircraft, the Buccaneer eventually became a valuable part of the RAF's strike force.

Right: A Buccaneer with a selection of weaponry carried by the aircraft. Most notable by its absence is the WE.177 tactical nuclear bomb, for many years the Buccaneer's primary weapon.

Right: The Buccaneer also played a major part in the RAF's Gulf War operations, acting as a laser designator aircraft for Tornado bombing missions.

Left: Shortly before their retirement a small number of Buccaneers had emerged from routine servicing with a new overall light grey colour scheme, deemed to be better suited to maritime operations.

Right: A night shot of a Buccaneer buried inside its HAS at Lossiemouth.

Left: With 'everything down' a Buccaneer poses for the camera over the Moray Firth. The huge air intakes for the Spey turbofans are particularly evident.

Lower left: Entering a tight turn to port, a Buccaneer of No. 208 Squadron reveals its underside and a Martel anti-radiation missile mounted beneath the port wing.

Below: Unlike other RAF strike/attack units, the Buccaneer maritime squadrons maintained a 'buddy-buddy' aerial refuelling capability which has been passed on to their Tornado replacements, although the facility has yet to be reintroduced.

Above: Proudly wearing the black-and-white checks of No. 43 Squadron, this Phantom FG.1 is resplendent in 1970s-style grey/green camouflage.

Above: Although they were purchased from the USA as an addition to the RAF's existing Phantom fleet, the F-4Js operated by No. 74 Squadron were, in effect, completely different aircraft, with American avionics and engines.

Bolow: A No. 1435 Flight Phantom FGR.2 assigned to the air defence of the Falkland Islands. This role is now undertaken by Tornado F.3s.

Top right: A No. 111 Squadron Phantom FG.1 on exercise with a Canberra T.17A of No. 360 Squadron in 1988.

Bottom right: In the air together for the last time, No. 74 Squadron's Phantom FGR.2s carefully formate to enable their tail code letters to spell 'TIGERS'.

Top left: To celebrate of the end of the Phantom's successful RAF career and the disbandment of No. 74 Squadron, one Phantom received the 'tiger treatment' in recognition of the unit's membership of the Nato tiger fraternity.

Bottom left: A Phantom FGR.2 of No. 56 Squadron during a CAP sortie over the North Sea in March 1989.

Top right: The de Havilland Devon served as a communications aircraft until the 1980s, when BAe 125s assumed this task. The example illustrated was retained by the BBMF as a crew transport.

Centre right: The BAe 125 was introduced to replace the RAF's Devon communications fleet. One is seen here in company with an Andover E.3 in 1989. The aircraft has now been partially withdrawn from service.

Right: The BAe 125 fleet received a low-visibility grey colour scheme before a rationalisation of the communications/light-transport fleet. The small number of 125s remaining in service are now assigned to No. 32 (Royal) Squadron, this unit having been combined with what was the Queen's Flight.

Above: A BAe 146 of No. 32 (Royal) Squadron, resplendent in its pristine patriotic colour scheme.

Below: The English Electric Canberra was the world's first jet bomber, and through the late 1950s and into the 1960s it formed the basis of the RAF's medium bomber force. When they were withdrawn from bomber operations, Canberras were assigned to a variety of second-line duties, as illustrated by this TT.18 target tug flown by No. 100 Squadron.

Above: Another second-line duty performed by the Canberra was ECM training. Canberra T.17s acted as enemy invaders, providing realistic disruption for RAF fighter pilots.

Below: At least one example of the T.4 two-seat dual-control version of the Canberra was assigned to every RAF Canberra squadron for continuation training.

Top: The PR.9 is an extensively modified version of the Canberra with larger wings, uprated engines and a sophisticated array of reconnaissance equipment. It remains in service with No. 39 (1 PRU) Squadron at Marham.

Above: Although very much in the 'historic' category, the RAF's reconnaissance Canberras still give the Service an

outstanding high-level-reconnaissance capability, and seem destined to remain in service into the next century.

Right: The RAF's target facilities and ECM training commitments have now been transferred to FR Aviation Ltd, a civilian contractor which operates a fleet of Dassault Falcons out of Newcastle and Bournemouth to meet the RAF's requirements.

Basic and Advanced Training

Left: The ungainly frontal aspect of a Jet Provost T.5 on the ramp at RAF Finningley, Yorkshire. Primarily used for flying training, the 'JP' was also used by No. 6 FTS for high-speed navigator training.

Joining the ranks of the RAF's élite flyers begins at the RAF College at Cranwell, Lincolnshire, where candidates are initially selected for officer training. Those who complete the long and rigorous course will then begin their first 'hands-on' flying just a few miles from Cranwell at Barkston Heath, where Hunting Aviation operates a fleet of Slingsby T67M Fireflies on behalf of the RAF. These simple but sturdy light aircraft enable instructors from the Joint Elementary Flight Training School (JEFTS) to assess a student's potential for full flying training, thus avoiding the expense of 'weeding out' the less able pilots at a later stage.

Those who are successful will then be posted to Linton-on-Ouse in Yorkshire, where the RAF now concentrates all of its basic flying training activities. Here, the fledgling pilots will join students from University Air Squadrons (scattered around the United Kingdom, these operate three-year training courses for suitably-qualified university students, flying Scottish Aviation Bulldog T.1s), and begin their basic training on the Shorts Tucano, the RAF's relatively youthful turboprop trainer which replaced the venerable Hunting Jet Provost.

The weeding process continues at Linton, of course, but most of the students who have progressed this far have fairly good flying abilities, and so the courses are geared more towards training rather than assessment. Even so, a surprising number o

Right: The RAF's Volunteer Gliding Schools provide inexpensive flying experience for Air Training Corps (ATC) cadets, operating a fleet of Grob Vigilant (illustrated), Viking, Valiant and Kestrel gliders.

Left: The Joint Elementary Flying Training School at Barkston Heath in Lincolnshire provides initial assessment and training for would-be RAF pilots. Their Slingsby Fireflies are operated on behalf of the RAF by Hunting Aviation.

Left: The recent amalgamation of the RAF's Air Experience Flights with University Air Squadrons has resulted in the retirement of the RAF's Chipmunks and a new regime of joint training on one aircraft type, the Scottish Aviation Bulldog T.1.

Left: The University Air Squadrons provide basic flying experience for university students wishing to pursue either flying or RAF service as a career. Traditionally, a substantial number of the RAF's pilots have been attracted from UASs.

students still face the 'chop' at some stage. The students who survive the Tucano training syllabus are then deemed fit to begin advanced training at RAF Valley in Anglesey, flying a fast and relatively sophisticated aircraft in the shape of the British Aerospace Hawk T.1A operated by Nos. 19(R), 74(R) and 208(R) Squadrons, all component squadrons of No. 4 Flying Training School (FTS).

One of Valley's Qualified Flying Instructors (QFIs) outlines the role of No. 4 FTS:

'We now have a combined syllabus, although the students are effectively doing the same training that they would have previously done with two separate units. Now the whole process is concentrated at one base, and even though the courses have changed somewhat, the training is much the same. There is a very clear-cut division between the advanced flying training and the tactical training elements of the course, but I have to say that the distinction between the two is gradually disappearing. It is very important that we keep the students on a learning curve. The advanced flying skills obviously have to be properly learned before we introduce the tactical training, so we have basically joined the two courses together rather than mixing them.

'Even when the student has progressed to tactical flying there are still a few general handling sorties slotted into the course anyway, so the new training system is fairly mixed, but at least the whole process is now concentrated on one airfield and the student is working within a more clearly defined learning curve. The student comes to Valley after having successfully mastered the basic flying skills required to fly the Tucano turboprop trainer. By the time he leaves here, he will have learned how to fly the Hawk jet trainer, how to drop bombs and how to fly air-combat sorties. The flying hours within the course are slightly reduced compared with the older system, but we have not removed anything of significance. Because the students are not required to change stations after completing the advanced flying phase, we do not need to fly any familiarisation sorties, so we can save some hours on duplication. Even so, we have lost one or two sorties from the course, but only really within the training element, so we still place great emphasis on thorough training. We have anticipated a drop in the number of students coming through here, but we are not working any less than we ever did before. Basically, we are talking about smaller courses in the future, to reflect the reduced commitments of the RAF's front-line squadrons.

'The students all fly the same course and really there is no distinction between the potential bomber or fighter pilot. We do not divide them into two distinct categories like we used to a few years ago, and now they all do the same combined course. At the very end we will decide where to post them. There are advantages to this system, as aircraft like the Harrier GR.7 and Tornado GR.1 are capable of flying air combat, even if only as part of a self-defence manoeuvre, so we think it is important that the student should have a good understanding of everyone's role, and that is bound to be of benefit when he begins flying an operational aircraft type.

'When the student leaves Valley, it is fair to say that he will have learned more than just the basics. He will certainly have learned how to lead an advanced air-defence sortie, using a ground intercept controller, using Sidewinder missiles and so on. Likewise, he will have learned how to lead a Simulated Attack Profile [SAP], flying an attack profile against a pre-briefed target, with one of our aircraft acting as an enemy fighter, trying to throw the bombers off course. That is a very demanding kind of sortie, so by the time he has finished the course he is going to be pretty capable.

'When he leaves here and moves to an Operational Conversion Unit, that is another quantum leap, at least in terms of the type of aircraft he is flying. It is often said that the Tornado is just like a big Hawk, and in many respects it is, but only in the same way that a bus is just a big van. The operating constraints are very different, and he will be flying in bigger formations of maybe six or eight aircraft, flying much further from base, and refuelling from tankers, so things are much more complicated, and the learning curve certainly does not stop as soon as he leaves here.'

Any students arriving at Valley with notions of becoming Tom Cruise Top Gun characters will quickly find their illusions shattered, as Valley is no place for actors. The emphasis is on old-fashioned hard work. The syllabus is very tough, and not every student will succeed. In fact, quite a few will be 'chopped' long before the course is completed. Those who are successful will be posted to an Operational

Left: Although it is still regarded as an excellent aircraft, the Bulldog's future with the RAF is uncertain, and future UAS students and ATC cadets may well find themselves flying in aircraft provided by civilian contractors.

Left: A Slingsby Firefly on short finals to Barkston Heath, with a student at the controls.

Conversion Unit (OCU), where they will learn how to fly one of the RAF's front-line operational aircraft. In the case of attack pilots these are the Panavia Tornado GR.1, British Aerospace Harrier GR.7 or SEPECAT Jaguar GR.1. By the time the students leave Valley they will have already become accomplished combat pilots. Towards the end of their course the students will be required to fly an SAP sortie. This fairly arduous task is essentially a simulation of a real combat mission, the aim of which is to deliver weapons accurately on to a designated target at a designated time.

The request for any given attack sortie will usually come in the form of an Air Task Message (ATM). This, together with a target photograph (when available), the intelligence officer's briefing, the ground liaison officer's (GLO's) briefing and the meteorological forecast, will provide all the information necessary to plan a mission. Among other things, the ATM will include full details of the task, the time on target (TOT), the positions of friendly forces, the number and type of weapons to be employed, and the number of aircraft to be used. The intelligence briefing will include details of surface-to-air missile

Right: The Folland Gnat was operated in the advanced flying training role by No. 4 FTS at Valley. Additionally, the type was flown by the Central Flying School, and their most famous component squadron, the Red Arrows, flew the type until it re-equipped with Hawks.

Right: The Yellowjacks team of No. 4 FTS were the forerunners of the famous Red Arrows. Following retirement from RAF service, this Gnat T.1 was repainted in the team's distinctive colour scheme.

Left: The venerable de Havilland Chipmunk has finally been retired from RAF service. This nostalgic view shows an Elementary Flying Training School 'Chippie' high over RAF Swinderby, Lincolnshire. Sadly, the aircraft, unit and base are now gone.

(SAM) and anti-aircraft-artillery (AAA) positions, target information gleaned from previous attacks or reconnaissance photographs, enemy radar coverage, and escape/evasion tactics, including search-and-rescue (SAR) cover. For most close-air-support (CAS) missions (relatively short-range 'battlefield' missions), a briefing would also be given by an Army GLO, providing details of radio frequencies being used, control agencies, callsigns, the position and description of contact points and Initial Points (IPs – from which the bombing runs can be calculated), the position of both friendly and enemy forces, the type of target marking in use (if any), and also the position of entry and exit 'gates' in

the area. Finally, the meteorological briefing will explore the weather conditions at base and in the target area, also looking at the locations of diversion airfields and their status, the en-route weather, winds, and contrail heights if any high-level flying is to be performed. All of this information will be presented to the student in a realistic manner, as part of his SAP preparation.

Working back from the TOT, the student is expected to decide how much time can be devoted to planning and briefing. The target photographs and maps need to be studied carefully, and an attack plan has to be established, using all the tactics employed by operational pilots. He may then allocate some

Below: Just one Chipmunk remains with the RAF, providing 'taildragger' experience for pilots of the Battle of Britain Memorial Flight (BBMF).

Right: One of the most famous postwar RAF trainers, the Vickers Varsity was used extensively by the RAF through the 1960s, primarily for navigation training. This example belonged to the RAF's Meteorological Research Flight, based at Farnborough, which now operates a Hercules W.2 research aircraft from Boscombe Down.

Below: The Hunting Jet Provost, of which a T.3A is seen at right and a T.5A at left, was the RAF's basic trainer through the 1960s and 1970s, and thousands of RAF students earned their wings on the type.

tasks to other members of the squadron, one person being responsible for 'domestics' (local air traffic procedures and so on), another looking at meteorological information, another dealing with route planning and map preparation, and another making fuel calculations. In many respects, as leader of the SAP, he is the 'manager' of the whole mission.

The planning sequence has to be arranged carefully, otherwise the time taken to plan the sortie can become unnecessarily protracted. For a typical SAP mission an instructor will provide the student with a target selected from a range of some 60 potential sites situated in the United Kingdom, mostly in Wales and Scotland.

These targets are familiar to the instructors as being easily recognisable, with good topographical features which make them ideal simulated targets. Naturally, it would be pointless to allocate an obscure target which the student would be unlikely to find. The instructor provides all the relevant data, as if the student was receiving a real ATM, and the student is then left to assemble the SAP based on this information. First he plans the met and intelligence briefings, and then he draws up suitable maps on a low-level 1:500,000-scale Ordnance Survey map, together with an even larger-scale (1:50,000) map which covers the more detailed IP-to-target phase of the mission. This document is

vital to the mission's success, giving the pilot a second-by-second countdown of the route towards the target.

The route to and from the target area is chosen by the student, and he will have many considerations to bear in mind when deciding this. Firstly, the simulated weapons which are being carried will require a specific type of delivery profile, and this will affect the direction and height from which the target is attacked. The target's defences will obviously vary in both quantity and quality, and the approach path must be designed to keep the aircraft masked from the defences for as long as possible, although the pilot will still need sufficient time to acquire the target visually and line up his sights on it. The number of aircraft in the formation also needs to be taken into account. It would be unwise to steer through a narrow valley with three other Hawks formating off your wingtips. The

terrain surrounding the target is an important factor, too, as well as the weather conditions, and the possibilities for re-attacking from another direction.

The best aiming point on the target must be chosen, in order to obtain the most destructive effects with the chosen weapon. Likewise, the sun's position also plays an important part in planning, as the tactic of 'diving out of the sun' is just as valid as it was in the First World War (the sun's position can also assist in finding the target). The effects of wind strength and direction must also be considered. The IP-to-target run is another vital consideration which requires careful planning. The IP is an easily-recognisable ground feature, chosen by the student, which must be between five and ten miles from the target. It also needs to be undefended and suitably positioned to allow the student to change maps roughly 30

Above: RAF Scampton's flight line, circa 1989. The Jet Provosts are long since retired, and Scampton has been virtually abandoned by the RAF. This aerial view reveals the outline of the huge dispersals originally built for Scampton-based Avro Vulcan bombers.

Above: 'Break, break, go.' A pair of JPs turn to port and starboard for the camera. Many Jet Provosts have been purchased by civilian operators, and can be seen around the world providing hours of (expensive) airborne pleasure.

seconds from the target. If all goes to plan, the student will directly overfly the IP on the target heading, using his large-scale map (with distances marked out in 10-second intervals) to make the final attack run. Although he will endeavour to be on track and on time as he overflies the IP, this will be his last opportunity to adjust his speed and direction if necessary, to fine-tune the attack.

Most SAP missions are planned to be 'lo-lo-lo'; low-level transit to the target, low-level attack and low-level return. This has to be considered when planning the sortie, as low-level flying will use much more fuel than a high-level route. Consequently, the target's location, the positioning of defences, the weather, combat fuel allowance (i.e. fuel to 'mix it' with defending fighters) and recovery fuel will all have to be taken into account, as will the location of built-up areas such as major cities. Smaller avoidance areas such as

farms, hospitals and so on will normally be treated as SAM or AAA sites, and avoided accordingly. The route to the target will also use the surrounding terrain to mask the formation from enemy radar wherever possible, although the safety constraints of a minimum height of 250ft have to be observed at all times. (In a real attack, any height at which the pilot felt confident could be chosen.) Likewise, terrain features will also help in navigation, and obvious features will be chosen for visual confirmation that the aircraft are flying on precisely the right track.

Most importantly, the student is advised to plan for the unexpected. For example, a delayed take-off might require an alternative (shorter) route to the target, and bad weather en route or at the target area might necessitate an alternative attack profile. Excessive fuel consumption might cause a change in route, and loss of contact with other aircraft in the formation (through bad weather or unserviceability) might demand a drastic rethinking of tactics. Worse still for the student, the SAP is sure to include a 'bounce', meaning that one of the instructors will chase the formation and intercept it without any warning, as if he were an enemy fighter, attempting to throw the aircraft off their intended route. The student has to defend himself and avoid becoming so distracted that he fails to hit his target. Navigational errors are always possible, and all students are tempted to pay such close attention to their route navigation that they fail to keep an eye open for marauding 'enemy fighters'. Instructors

constantly try to emphasise that a good lookout is vital, and the 'bounce' aircraft is a very effective way of demonstrating what will happen if the student spends too much time looking at his map. Planning is all-important, and the mission will succeed or fail depending on how well the student prepares, before he even climbs into his aircraft.

The following is an extract from an SAP briefing; the student talking:

'We will go as a pair, pushing out to battle formation for transit, and then we will close up for our descent into Shawbury. That will be a full radar-to-visual approach to

Left: Hawker Siddeley Dominie navigation trainers on the ramp at RAF Finningley. Following the closure of Finningley, the Dominies have relocated to Cranwell as No. 55(R) Squadron.

overshoot and then depart at low level. If I see any opportunities to cut corners we shall take them; otherwise we will fly straight down Shawbury's extended centreline. It is flight level one-seven-zero to Shawbury, and we expect to be on runway two-three-three. Formation is battle, and flying wing as required. For recovery we will split for individual visual recoveries back here. Bird strike, we will go as a pair and I prefer to be pushed, so I would be up front there. Low level, we are heading one-two-zero, climbing through the airways into Shawbury for a fast-speed radar-to-visual. A 300-knot transit, and as soon as we are Victor Mike [visual met conditions] with the ground we will

overshoot and depart on one-six-zero until we are clear of Low-Flying Area [LFA] Nine, descending to low level. What have we got by way of visuals?

'OK, we have an enormous two-thirty-nine double mast here just by the railway line, and this tip of land with a two-ten mast on, and then sliding down the ridge we have a pair of six-seventy-foot masts. We do not want to hit them, so we want to be about a mile to the right of them. Then we are starting to pick up the woods and we are time hacking on the lake in the woods just on the edge of LFA Nine. Down past Bridgnorth and we obviously cannot stray left. Keep an eye open for any civvies [civil aircraft]

Right: Although it is a relatively old aircraft, the Dominie is undergoing a refit programme, emerging as an all-new navigation trainer equipped with systems more appropriate to the RAF's latest front-line aircraft.

bumbling into Halfpenny Green. We are looking to pick up the dam and the woods which feed into the bigger woods to turn on to the IP.

'We will come off the target on one-six-six down to the woods and low ground around Bromyard, to pick up the distinctive ridge and the Wellington sheds complex, to turn on to our IP. Off target we will miss Ross-on-Wye and pick up the motorway, turning to come across the top of Abergavenny – fifteen-ninety-five spot height is a good lead there – and, if we need to go south of Abergavenny, watch those red spots to avoid. Turning up the valley towards Brecon, we turn short of Brecon into fighting wing formation if necessary, but maintaining battle [formation] if we can. It is an air threat throughout, so I want you looking at my six o'clock all the time. Round we go, and we have got Senny-bridge mast. Llandrindod Wells, and we are

starting to think about pulling up to save some gas, and then it is three-four-zero from Newtown, back to Valley.

'So, the first target is on two-one-five, at 36 seconds from the IP. There is a reservoir to lead us in, the woods abeam, looking ahead in the two-o'clock position for the next set of woods. Down past Highley and my IP is Maxfields Coppice, and you will be making a 4g turn through 90° to get yourself behind me. Now, looking ahead, I have the wood to the left and the town on the right side, but I want to be looking for the valley line, which will hopefully be quite distinctive. Then I am looking for the wiggle in the river and then the railway line, leading us to the bridge and the complex at the target. If you look where the railway line is, I think I should be able to see where the railway crosses the river. So we are looking for the big bridge beyond the house for our target.'

Above: The Service's latest basic trainer, the Shorts Tucano T.1, is the aircraft in which the RAF teaches students the rudimentary skills of military flying.

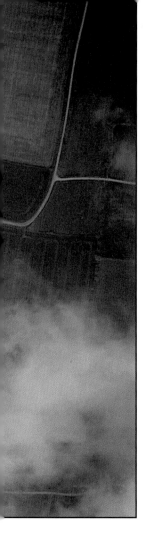

Right: Wearing Cranwell's distinctive blue band, a Tucano T.1 flies high over Lincolnshire before the relocation of the Tucano fleet to Linton-on-Ouse.

Left: A typical pilot's-eye view of a Tucano tail chase, with the all-important instructor's stopwatch prominent in the centre of the picture.

The briefing continues, covering further target details and a complete description of the second target which is included in the SAP mission. After almost an hour the briefing will be complete and the aircrew are ready to walk to their aircraft after collecting their flying gear and 'signing' for their mounts. Out on the flightline the conditions are not always as glamorous as one might expect. This is not a movie, and it is no time to make a Tom Cruise-style walk down the line. The weather is terrible, with driving rain and fierce winds, and the only sensible thing to do is to get inside the aircraft as quickly as possible. However, the external walk-round checks have to be completed first, while the ground crew are busy shovelling away the pool of water which has rapidly collected inside the Hawk's canopy. With the checks complete, the crew can climb into the rain-soaked cockpits, strapping in before the canopies are quickly closed. Once the rainwater has been wiped from the instrument faces, the start-up sequence gets under way, and in just a few minutes the Hawk's Roll-Royce/Turboméca Adour turbofan is quietly turning at idle speed.

After taxying to the active runway, the two-ship formation ('Bobcat One' and 'Bobcat Two') rolls on to the threshold and takes up position in line abreast, running engines up to full power. Although the Adour creates a considerable amount of noise, the conditions inside the Hawk are fairly comfortable, and all that can be heard through one's 'bonedome' is a distant rumble, accompanied by a gentle airframe shudder. With a nod from the lead pilot (to cue the brake release for the wingman), the Hawk lurches forward and quickly begins to accelerate along Valley's runway. At 90kt the control column is moved slightly rearwards, raising the Hawk's nose into the airstream. At 120kt the stick is rotated further and the Hawk is airborne, accompanied by the wingman, both aircraft bobbing and weaving in the turbulent conditions. At 150ft the landing gear is retracted and the flaps are then raised, the pilot ensuring that they are fully up before he reaches 200kt.

After climbing through the cloud, the Hawks are positioned in battle formation, separated by about a mile. The high-level transit enables them to reach a suitable

Above: Looking particularly smart in its new all-black 'high-vis' colour scheme, this Shorts Tucano T.1 is from No. 1 FTS, Linton-on-Ouse.

'entry gate' into a low-level route without wasting fuel unnecessarily. With the assistance of a radar controller 'Bobcat' formation is guided through the clouds towards RAF Shawbury, where the formation leader descends into the low-level phase of the mission after making visual contact with the ground. Back under the cloud cover, the two Hawks level off at 250ft, driving through the heavy rain, banging and rocking as they hit continual pockets of turbulence. The conditions are terrible, and occasional patches of thick, low-level cloud create further hazards, forcing the formation to make detours and adding to the students' navigational problems.

After passing to the right of Telford on a heading of 160° the formation approaches the first IP, and at a speed of 420kt the student does not have much time to locate its position. With a 4g turn to starboard the

aircraft are positioned on a heading of 215°, passing directly over the IP towards the target. Just 36 seconds later the target bridge flashes by, partly obscured by thick trees. Fortunately the formation leader had successfully identified the target and positioned the Hawk on a perfect simulated 1,000lb high-explosive (retarded) bombing approach, quickly followed by 'Bobcat Two'. Attacks such as this demonstrate that target acquisition is incredibly difficult, although level attacks do make sighting somewhat easier. With a fixed approach altitude the pilot can simply wait until the target fills the appropriate amount of his bomb sight.

Once clear of the target, both aircraft turn hard on to 166° for a further two minutes before turning right on to 255°. Due south of Leominster another turn is made, this time on to the next target heading of 155°, passing over the IP at 420kt and still at 250ft.

Above: In this view with the gear extended, the Tucano's large canopy is evident, giving both instructor and student excellent all-round visibility.

Left: Although it is turboprop powered, the Tucano has a performance roughly similar to that of its predecessor, the Jet Provost, though operating costs in terms of fuel usage are much lower.

One minute and eight seconds from the IP the lead pilot pulls up to begin a dive attack, turning right through 60° at the top of the climb before establishing himself on a 10° dive at the second target, which in this case is another bridge.

The weapons to be used in any attack will normally be predetermined by a higher authority, and three basic types are available. These are the 1,000lb high-explosive retarded bomb, which is used to best effect against bridges, dams, or other hardened buildings; the cluster bomb unit (CBU) used against armour, radar installations, aircraft on the ground or troop concentrations; and the cannon, used primarily against 'soft' vehicles, aircraft and rail facilities or for flak suppression. Each weapon type is simulated during the student's training course, although the cannon is only used as an option when operating over a weapons range, where both live bombs and live ammunition can be used. The type of weapon carried will directly influence the tactics of the mission. Some weapons, such as cannon, rockets and unretarded bombs, must be fired or delivered in a dive, whereas the CBU and retarded bombs offer the choice of a dive or a level attack. The type of weapon will also determine the tip-in attitude, and its accuracy and damage pattern on the ground will affect the attack direction.

The basic aim of each pilot is to maximise the time available for target acquisition and weapons accuracy, but at the same time minimise the aircraft's exposure to enemy defences; contradictory considerations requiring compromise. On the Hawk, the recommended profile is to pull up from low level to achieve the required 10° dive angle and turn through 40–80° (ideally 60°) on to the attack heading. The standard operating procedure (SOP) distances give a reasonable compromise of minimum exposure time and acceptable tracking and acquisition time. As with the level attack, an untrained observer will find a dive attack both confusing and disorientating, although it is naturally much easier to acquire the target visually once the

Right, upper and lower: Operating Scottish Aviation Jetstream T.1s from Cranwell, No. 45(R) Squadron is responsible for multi-engine training. Tasked primarily with training duties, the unit also undertakes light transport duties as and when required.

aircraft is positioned on the final attack dive.

Pulling up from the target, 'Bobcat Two' streaks in behind 'Bobcat One' to complete the simulated attack, turning hard right on to 260°. The ride is still rough, the weather still poor, but provided the low-level visibility is adequate the SAP continues as planned. The RAF instructors recognise that operational missions are unlikely to afford the luxury of clear skies, and that it is therefore important to make training as realistic as possible. After climbing out of the low-level route, 'Bobcat One' and 'Bobcat Two' make their way back to Valley at high level, descending over Bettws-y-Coed to run in over the airfield at 2,000ft and 250kt (the finals turn speed), and the touchdown is made at just over 110kt.

After taxying back to the flightline the crews gather for a debriefing, during which the instructor examines every aspect of the sortie in detail, concentrating on those things that the student can improve upon. The instructor for the sortie flown by 'Bobcat One' and 'Bobcat Two' is suitably impressed:

'He is a very good student. He was working really hard all around the cloudy areas, and the first target was a very difficult one. We had a little confusion at one stage, but he did very well. He is fine. I would say that the mission was better than average. It is not unusual to miss the targets sometimes, and that is OK, as it is all a learning process. If the targets were easy ones and the student repeatedly missed them we would naturally be concerned. So much would depend on why the student missed them. But by using hard targets we are able to prove that the navigation and acquisition techniques are working.

'Towards the end of the course the students are learning to do everything as a pair of aircraft. They could do that SAP sortie easily on their own, but when they are a pair,

Below: The British Aerospace Hawk T.1A is the RAF's advanced jet trainer. This 1987 study shows an aircraft in the early red, white and grey colour scheme then common to all RAF training aircraft.

and the students are coordinating two aircraft, it gets tricky. Sometimes things tend to start happening too quickly, and the student has to think ahead. Organising two aeroplanes flying in battle formation can be like trying to handle an unstoppable train, and it takes a great deal of effort to keep everyone going in the right direction. Navigation is becoming almost second nature by now; everything tends to degrade, so he has to work even harder.

'When we talk about capacity we mean the ability to "prioritise". For example, he has to realise when he has to look at the map to avoid getting lost, or decide when he should be telling his wingman what to do, and so on. Capacity is vitally important, and if he cannot cope with everything that is going on at the same time, then he is in trouble. Sometimes the student simply cannot navigate well at low level, but we can teach anyone if they have the capacity to learn. We

tend to lose maybe just one or so students on each course, but by this stage we tend to have weeded out most of the students who cannot handle the job. We lost a student recently. He was unable to think in three dimensions – just had not got the capacity to cope – so we dropped him, but he will be offered a flying post on helicopters or transports in all probability.

'Although the air force is contracting, we have not been encouraged to be more selective, and we teach in the same way as we always have. Additionally, the new combined syllabus does not affect the students in any way. Much of the training is done within the OCU, however, so there is no point covering everything in the advanced and tactical training course. For example, the Hawk's bomb sight obviously is not used on the Tornado, Jaguar or Harrier, so some of the training will naturally have to be done within the OCUs.

Below: Seen during a training sortie from RAF Valley, these two No. 4 FTS Hawks illustrate the unit's more recent livery, which introduced dark blue to produce a very distinctive (and patriotic) colour scheme.

Above: At the time of the Hawk's entry into RAF service, advanced training was divided into flying and tactical phases, with Tactical Weapons Units (TWUs) specifically geared towards the teaching of weapons delivery tactics. RAF Chivenor in Devon was the home of Nos. 63 and 151 Squadrons, assigned to this role.

Below: Hawks were also modified to carry Sidewinder AAMs to provide the RAF with short-range air defence which could be used in conjunction with Tornadoes in a wartime scenario. Although training for this wartime role is now greatly reduced, Hawks retain their fighter capability.

'The course here at Valley is different now, but it has not lost much, other than maybe a couple of sorties. So far as the students are concerned things have not really changed since the Tactical Weapons Units disappeared. The course here at Valley is identical to that provided by Chivenor, prior to that unit's closure, although Valley is 80 miles from the weapons range at Pembrey, whereas Chivenor is only 60 miles away, so we did take the students to Chivenor for three weeks on detachment for the weapons phase of the course while the base was still active. Now all the sorties are flown directly from Valley. The students now fly camouflaged or black aircraft right from the beginning of their advanced training, and they will see people in their crew room who are actually doing the tactical weapons flying, so they feel that little bit closer to the action. We have moved away from the red-and-white-trainer attitude, and that must give the students the right kind of impression, right from the start!'

Right: An instructor's view through the gunsight of a Hawk T.1A during a low-level training sortie over snow-covered Wales.

Right: Following the amalgamation of advanced and tactical training, all of the RAF's Hawk training operations are now concentrated at Valley, from where low-level missions over sparsely-populated Wales can be easily conducted.

Above: The ever-popular sight of the glorious Red Arrows getting smartly airborne to begin another breathtaking routine.

Below: Back on the ground, the nine-strong team returns to the flight line to begin a video-aided debrief in its headquarters at Scampton. The team has now relocated to Cranwell, although many practice sorties are still flown over Scampton.

Below right: The world-famous Red Arrows regularly 'borrow' Hawks from Valley to enable them to continue display practice during the winter months, when many of their own aircraft are being overhauled. This example from No. 234 Squadron (now disbanded) wears a bizarre mix of training colours and TWU markings, and carries a Red Arrows smoke pod.

Above: Partly to reflect the Hawk's air defence role the grey/green camouflage applied to TWU Hawks was replaced by air defence grey colours, as illustrated by this dolphin-like example from No. 63 Squadron, seen low over the Bristol Channel.

Above: As part of an attempt to improve flight safety, the RAF has identified gloss black as the most eye-catching 'colour' for its training fleet. Consequently the colourful red, white and grey aircraft are now reappearing in a smart black scheme, seen here on No. 74(R) Squadron's specially decorated 'tiger' aircraft.

Left: An unusual aerial view of the Red Arrows as they perform over Scampton. Although the RAF has vacated the base, Scampton still provides airspace for the team to practise many of its routines.

Left: RAF St Athan operates a pair of Hawks as part of its Tornado servicing commitment. Ferry crews are often flown to or from the RAF's Tornado bases in these Hawks, one of which wears a beautiful Welsh dragon motif along its fuselage.

Front Line Training

Having successfully completed the course at Valley, students move on to begin training on a front-line combat aircraft type. For pilots destined to fly in the strike/attack role, this means the Harrier, Tornado or Jaguar. One of three Jaguar units stationed at Coltishall in Norfolk is No. 54 Squadron, RAF. It is allocated to NATO's Allied Command Europe (ACE) Mobile Force, and its primary role had been to support, from bases in Denmark, NATO's northern flank in the event of a war with the now-defunct Warsaw Pact. However, following the break-up of the Soviet Union,

the RAF's Jaguars have been employed in different roles; not least during Operation Desert Storm during the Gulf War, when they were operated very successfully without incurring a single loss.

Jaguars remain in the Middle East, a presence being maintained in Turkey. Low running costs, ease of deployment and high reliability were all factors which favoured the Jaguar, and, contrary to earlier plans for its early replacement by the European Fighter Aircraft (EFA), it will remain in RAF service for some time, following a decision first to re-equip the RAF's Tornado F.3 squadrons with EFAs

Below: A Jaguar GR.1 wearing the markings of No. 6 Squadron receives a tractor tow to a static engine test.

Above: Jaguars on No. 226 OCU's ramp at Lossiemouth. The aircraft in the foreground wears the light grey colour scheme applied to some Jaguars during the mid-1990s.

Above left: RAF Jaguars played a significant part in the Gulf War. One such veteran of the conflict is seen here at Scampton, complete with nose art and mission markings.

(although this is probably an indication of the RAF's regard for the Tornado F.3, rather than an eagerness to retain the Jaguar indefinitely).

Coltishall is home to two other Jaguar squadrons, Nos. 6 and 41, while No. 16(R) Squadron at Lossiemouth acts as the Jaguar OCU (and is expected to move south to Coltishall eventually). Each squadron is equipped largely with single-seat GR.1As, although small numbers of two-seat T.2As are also operated (the majority with the OCU) for check rides, dual control instruction, etc. The GR.1A is primarily a ground-attack aircraft, although some export models of the Jaguar are employed as air defence fighters.

At present, approximately twelve aircraft are assigned to No. 54 Squadron, together with sixteen pilots. The number and type of missions flown each week depend largely

Right: A close-up of a 'Desert Cat' Jaguar reveals an impressive number of mission markings and some patriotic artwork.

upon aircraft serviceability, and whether the squadron is working up to any major exercises. For example, a pilot can expect to fly 30 hours a month. A typical mission will last for roughly 90 minutes, unless the sortie includes air-to-air combat, in which case the duration drops significantly to around 40 minutes because of the thirsty characteristics of the Jaguar's Rolls-Royce Adour engines when reheat is used.

The tasking for each mission is normally received two hours before the scheduled take-off time, the standard Nato timescale. The briefing begins with a time check, followed by the aims of the sortie, call-signs, a listing of the pilots, the aircraft serials, the weapons fit each aircraft is carrying and the aerodynamic limits to which each can be flown. Spare aircraft are detailed, together with the weather for the local and target

areas, the amount of fuel needed to return to base, and who will be responsible for making the various fuel calls and radio frequencies (which are pre-briefed to avoid the need to broadcast such details when in the air). The Jaguar is equipped with 'Have Quick' frequency-agile radios which are virtually resistant to jamming.

The briefing continues with details of the take-off, recovery, routes to be flown, heights, 'notams' (Notices to Airmen), royal flights, safety altitudes, emergencies, air-to-air refuelling (if it is to be employed) and so on. The evasion brief gives details of the types of aircraft which the Jaguar pilots will be avoiding, the limits to which evasion will be flown, and the tactics which are to be employed. The whole briefing will last up to 40 minutes, depending on the pilots' experience. If the formation includes a 'new boy', the brief will have to include precise details of what is going on, so that he is left in absolutely no doubt as to what is expected of him.

The planning for each mission is time-consuming, but it is vital to the success of each sortie. The Jaguar pilots adhere to a much-used acronym, 'Kiss' – keep it simple and safe. The target is first examined, and weapons are then assigned as appropriate, after which the ground crews will be advised of the weapons fit required for each aircraft. The route to the target is studied, threats are taken into account (with a great deal of input from an Army GLO assigned to the squadron), and the delivery techniques – level bombing, dive bombing, etc. – are chosen. The Jaguar is equipped with an FIN1064 inertial navigation system (INS), a very accurate system which runs a projected map display and generates steering information in the head-up display (HUD). If times for waypoints are programmed into the computer it will also give demanded ground speed and actual ground speed. This enables the pilot to arrive at his designated target precisely on time, provided he adheres strictly to the HUD information. The TOT is vitally important, to avoid conflict with other strikes, reconnaissance overflights or friendly manoeuvres on the ground.

Above: Jaguars taxy back to Coltishall's ramp after returning from the Gulf. Their temporarily-applied sand camouflage scheme was quickly removed.

Above: Illustrating what is now the definitive colour scheme for the Jaguar fleet (as well as the Tornado and Harrier offensive support squadrons), this aircraft carries the markings of No. 16(R) Squadron, the Jaguar OCU.

The INS requires specific details of the target, such as its latitude and longitude; its height, so that the HUD can generate a bar over the predicted target position before it becomes visible to the pilot; and the IP position, so that any 'wandering' by the INS can be updated between 30 and 90 seconds before the aircraft arrives at the target. Some pre-IP updates can also be fed into the INS, the most accurate means of revising the INS's data being to use the Jaguar's laser target seeker head, although this is strictly a wartime option, as the Jaguar's laser is not 'eye-safe'. Indeed, in peacetime the laser can be used only over weapons ranges, and only within a few hundred yards of the target position. The IP and target coordinates become two of a series of waypoints which form the complete route that is fed into the INS.

The RAF Jaguar fleet uses a total avionics briefing system (TABS) which enables the pilot to feed all the relevant data into the aircraft swiftly and easily. He lays his map on to a digitising map table and programmes each waypoint into a data store by means of a hand-held cursor. A TV monitor displays the information as it is programmed, enabling errors to be corrected as required. Once the route is properly programmed, the 32K-memory portable data store (PODS) is ready to be 'plugged' into the aircraft. A record of the flight is given to an operations officer, who will book the aircraft into the low-flying system and also into the necessary weapons ranges. Departure out of the airfield is also booked with air traffic control so that the Jaguars can be handed over to a radar control authority if required, although for many missions the aircraft will depart visually at low level.

Part of this planning must include careful timing of the attack phase, so that a first-run attack on a weapons range is timed to coincide with the operating periods at the range (which closes at various times to allow the targets to be replaced, etc.). Therefore the TOT and time on range must match. A formal flight plan is filed only if the aircraft are expected to enter the airways network or if they are flying overseas.

When planning is completed it is time to gather the appropriate flying kit, which includes the bulky immersion suit if sea temperatures are below 10° Celsius. An anti-g suit is worn, together with the usual gloves, life preserver and flying helmet. Once the pilot is fully kitted out it is time to 'walk', the next stop being the Operations Desk, where a final 'out brief' is given by the authorising officer. The crews then walk to the line hut to sign out each aeroplane (the usual RAF Form 700), checking that each machine is fuelled correctly, carrying the correct weapons fit, and fully serviceable. Unacceptable defects are always noted in red ('I always look for missing wings or wheels, and then start checking for the less obvious stuff,' comments one Jaguar pilot), and acceptable defects are also noted, these being regarded as relatively unimportant

provided the pilot is aware of them. Individual aircraft also develop specific problems which tend to recur, and each pilot is therefore very careful to note any previously-recorded defects in case they arise again during the flight.

Arriving at his aircraft, the pilot makes a preliminary inspection, ensuring that it is parked correctly, that chocks are fitted under the wheels, that safety pins are fitted to each weapon, that external equipment is available and that a fire extinguisher is present. He then climbs into the aircraft, checking that the cockpit's circuit breakers are all set and that the battery, ignition and parking brake are all on. The ejection-seat pins are confirmed as being fitted, and then the rudder pedals and the seat are adjusted as required by the individual. Looking to the left side of the cockpit, the pilot checks that the undercarriage handle is down, that the canopy jettison handle is flush and that the

Below: To mark No. 16(R) Squadron's 75th anniversary, this Jaguar was given an all-black colour scheme and large representations of the unit's markings. The saint refers to the fact that the unit was first formed at St Omer in France, while the crossed keys refer to its original reconnaissance role – unlocking the enemy's secrets.

arrester hook handle is fully forward. Behind each throttle is an igniter relight button, and a clicking sound will confirm that this is functioning correctly. The master armament safety bus bar key is then fitted into its slot, and the pilot climbs out of the aircraft again to complete his full external check of the aircraft.

His first task is to look into the nosewheel bay, where he selects a number of switches to indicate the weapons fit and the ballistic mode in which the weapons will be dropped. The AN/ALE-40 chaff and flare dispenser selections are also made in the nosewheel bay. The checks then continue with a look at the various vents, to ensure that they are all unblocked. The hydraulic accumulators are checked for the correct pressure, and the safety pins are all confirmed as being removed. On a more general note, the pilot will look for any leaks and, if necessary, check with an engineer that they are within certain

specified limits. He will also look for any loose panels and unusual cracks, check inside the engine intakes for the presence of any foreign objects, check the exhausts, confirming that the afterburner rings are in good condition and that the fuel shield inside the engine bay is not likely to fall off. Removal of the arrester hook pins and brake parachute pins is also checked.

The Jaguar has an internal starter unit incorporating a microswitch which needs to be placed in the correct position, and the starter's oil level is checked at the same time. It is also normal to see pilots shaking the various external stores on their pylons, ensuring that they are all properly secured. Once he is satisfied that his aircraft is in good condition, the pilot can climb back into the cockpit to complete the pre-start checks. Strapping in is the first task, however, working from left to right, attaching the personal equipment connector (for oxygen

Below: During the Gulf War, participating Jaguars were fitted with overwing missile rails enabling them to carry Sidewinder AAMs for self-protection. The capability was retained after the conflict, although missiles are rarely carried on day-to-day training missions.

Left: A Jaguar GR.1A from No. 41 Squadron at low level over the North York Moors.

Left: Banking away from the camera, a Jaguar of No. 41 Squadron reveals the centreline-mounted reconnaissance pod carried by the unit's aircraft. In addition to its primary reconnaissance role the squadron also flies offensive-support missions.

and anti-g air pressure), the personal survival pack (liferaft, flares, etc.), leg restraints, lap and shoulder straps, RT lead and helmet. He also removes the seat safety pins, after which the 'liney' (the flightline mechanic who assists the pilot with these procedures) will remove the access ladder.

Working from left to right again, almost every item of equipment in the cockpit is checked, starting with the wander lamps and autostabilisation systems (pitch, yaw and roll). The laser unit is also checked to ensure that it is switched off. The flaps are selected 'up', although without hydraulic pressure they will not actually move. The INS is normally switched on before the pilot climbs into the cockpit, to give the equipment plenty of time to warm up and align itself with the aircraft's position. The pilot plugs in his data pod and selects DTS (data transfer), checking that the route is programming into the computer properly. Throttles are checked for full and free movement, and the main flight instruments are all scrutinised to ensure that they are working properly. The HUD is turned on to the correct mode, usually 'Radalt' (radio altimeter) for take-off.

On the right-hand side of the cockpit are various fuel gauges and warning panels. The fuel cross-feeds are checked, as is the electro-hydraulic pump (EHP) which supplies hydraulic pressure if both pumps fail in flight. The engine instruments are examined, and then the alternators and transformer/rectification units are switched on. The air conditioning is switched to 'ground' and the tactical air navigation (Tacan) equipment is activated. It is now time to start the engines.

The pilot makes a hand signal to the ground crew, indicating that he is ready to run-up the microturbo starter, which takes roughly five seconds to spool up to 85 per cent power. Once the unit is steady at an idle setting, the pilot holds one finger vertically in the air, signalling that he is starting No. 1 engine. He opens the low-pressure cock and presses the start button. When the engine has wound up to around 52 per cent he checks that the various captions are off and that the flaps are raising themselves to the selected position. Then No. 2 engine is started and, once it is running satisfactorily, the external power is switched off. Each engine incorporates a dump valve which releases excess air from the compressor during start-up, and advancing the throttles to 61 per cent closes the bleed valves, this being confirmed by a slight reduction in the turbine gas temperature (TGT). The engines idle at between 54rpm and 57rpm while on the ground. The flying controls are checked. Flaps can be moved to one of eight settings, half flap being 20° and full flap 40°. The flaps and leading-edge slats run along the entire trailing and leading edges of the wing, and turning is achieved through the use of spoiler devices on the upper wings, rather than by the more conventional ailerons. For take-off the flaps are set at 20°.

Radio check-in with the rest of the formation begins at the pre-briefed time, the pilots using one of a pre-set range of twenty frequencies, Stud One being for ground operations (start-up and taxy). The INS is switched from the alignment mode, and nosewheel steering is selected by means of a switch on the control column which also operates cameras when the Jaguar is flying in the reconnaissance mode. The aircraft is now ready to taxy. With roughly 70 per cent power on each engine, the parking brake is released and the aircraft gently rolls forward. At this stage the pilot makes a stab on the footbrakes to check for pressure before returning the throttles to idle and turning left or right to avoid damaging other aircraft (or personnel) with jet blast.

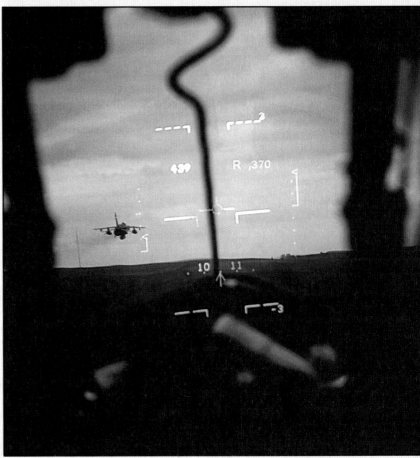

Left: Down among the weeds in a Jaguar, or, to be precise, 555ft, according to the HUD.

Left: Comfortably clearing the crest of a Cumbrian hillside: a Jaguar pilot's view through the HUD at 439kt.

While the pilot is taxiing to the active runway there is time to consider the various emergency procedures employed by Jaguar crews. If an engine should fail while the aircraft is on the take-off roll and still below 100kt forward speed, the take-off can simply be aborted by bringing the throttles back to idle and streaming the braking parachute. The aircraft will be very heavy, putting a great deal of strain on the undercarriage and brakes, but a safe stop can be achieved. If the aircraft is travelling faster than 100kt, the 'one-shot' arrester hook can be lowered (it has to be raised again externally by a member of the ground crew), and the aircraft will grab the overshoot cable as it approaches the end of the runway. Alternatively a single-engined take-off can be made, by raising the undercarriage and dumping all of the external stores by means of a single emergency switch. However, the pilot has to be careful not to dump any weapons on top of the travelling undercarriage. Speed is life as far as the Jaguar pilot is concerned, so the faster the aircraft flies, the lower the angle of attack (AOA) can be, and the aim on a single-engine take-off is primarily to achieve speed rather than altitude.

At the end of the runway the INS clock is started and the radio is changed to the control tower frequency, enabling the pilot to obtain departure instructions. The aircraft is then ready to line-up on the runway, with the other formation aircraft positioning themselves line-abreast. Four is the largest number of aircraft which can be manoeuvred in this manner. Once into position, each pilot checks the runway control caravan for any safety signals, checks that all warning captions in the cockpit are out, and checks that the INS clock is running. The throttles are then smoothly pushed up to full dry power while the aircraft is held on the footbrakes, the pilot looking to see that the

exhaust-gas temperature (EGT) remains within the limit of 700° Celsius.

With a thumbs-up signal from the wingman, the leader makes a chopping motion with his hand to signal brake release, and the aircraft begin their take-off roll, usually in pairs, or, in the case of a four-ship departure, a pair of pairs separated by 30 seconds (an equivalent of roughly three miles). Stream take-offs are more likely if there is a significant crosswind.

Another nod from the leader as his aircraft passes 40kt and the pilots release the catches on their throttles to free the afterburners, checking that the fuel flow increases, although the Adour engines are very reliable and faults seldom occur. At the pre-briefed rotation speed (dependent upon aircraft weight and ambient temperature, although it is usually around 180kt when heavy and 140kt when light) the aircraft is rotated through 14° AOA and the Jaguar is smartly airborne, normally having used about 5,000ft of runway from brake release.

Once airborne, the aircraft quickly move into formation positions, achieved by visually lining up tail units and wing positions. The undercarriage and flaps are raised, and the AOA audio warning and air conditioning are switched on. (Air conditioning drains 4 or 5 per cent thrust from the engines, so it is not used until after take-off.) The Jaguar is a sprightly performer when flown 'clean' (without any external stores), requiring only 2,000ft to take off, but for most missions a pair of 2,035lb external fuel tanks are carried, one under each wing. Moreover, the Adour engines do not perform very well in hot weather, and at extremes of 30° Celsius or more, with a full fuel load and weapons fit, the Jaguar requires at least 7,000ft of runway in which to get airborne. However, the engines can be modified for hot-weather operations, giving them additional thrust, and

RAF Jaguars were uprated in this way during Operation Desert Storm.

Establishing the aircraft on an initial outbound heading, the pilot now ensures that the aircraft's defensive systems are functioning, these being the electronic countermeasures (ECM), radar warning receiver (RWR) and chaff/flare dispensers. The formation will then adopt tactics appropriate to either a ground threat or an air threat, as necessary. The Jaguar's radar altimeter is considered very accurate (pilots confirm that it reads '5ft' when the aircraft is taxying), and this enables the aircraft to be flown at ultra-low levels when necessary. A mere 15ft above the sea is quite practical, the only real limits being the risk of scraping external stores on the surface or the nerve of the pilot. However, such low flying is reserved for operational circumstances, and for normal peacetime training in the United Kingdom the standard minimum height of 250ft applies, special permission for 100ft above ground level (AGL) flights occasionally being granted within specially designated areas.

Jaguars normally fly in battle formation, positioned line-abreast with a separation of between 2,000 and 3,000 yards to ensure that a hostile aircraft cannot close in on the six-o'clock position of any Jaguar without being spotted by a wingman. The entire formation can fly in a wide line-abreast position, or a four-ship flight can be split into pairs, the trailing pair forming a card formation. Low flying is still considered the key to survival in a hostile environment, even though the RAF's Jaguars operated mostly at medium altitudes over Iraq and Kuwait during Desert Storm. The Allied air forces were able to establish air supremacy over the area, creating a 'sterile' environment in which the attack aircraft could operate without any risk of interception by enemy fighters. This enabled pilots to use medium heights for attack profiles, but as the same kind of benign air environment is unlikely to exist elsewhere, the RAF has not drastically revised flying training policies as a result of that conflict.

The Jaguar's high wing loading makes it a good performer at low level, giving the pilot a very safe and smooth ride with no smoke trail and a fairly small radar cross-section. Indeed, during any period of concentrated low-level, contour-hugging flying, the Jaguar can literally zoom into valleys, climb up the hillside and then be rolled through 180° to pull sharply down the next hillside back into another valley. This technique keeps the aircraft under positive g at all times, rather than the usual more gentle 'bunt' over each hill which would make the aircraft more vulnerable to detection. Naturally, this kind of flying requires great skill and a good knowledge of the terrain if it is to be done safely. Likewise, the Jaguar needs to be flown fairly light to achieve this kind of manoeuvring. A fully fuelled and bombed-up aircraft could not be thrown around with such force; a full weapons load significantly reduces the aircraft's roll rate, for instance.

As the aircraft reaches each designated turning point, the HUD changes to a loose navigation mode and a marker appears over the predicted position of the waypoint. As the aircraft flies over the waypoint the pilot will update the INS position if necessary and select the 'change destination' button, switching the HUD back to navigation mode. Some 60 seconds from the all-important IP the INS will display a cue on the HUD. The pilot will then check his bomb selection, and check that the pylons are activated and that the weapons are fused. He also checks the 'stick spacing' (the interval between each bomb drop), and selects an 'auto attack' by computer or a manual attack, and guns on or off. The late arm safety switch is then selected to make the whole system live. Finally, a small catch on top of the control column is activated, enabling the computer to drop the bombs at the required time. Targets are usually acquired visually, although the laser system can be used to give a suitable cue on the HUD.

For an automatic attack the pilot will place a target bar over the target position, using a small controller unit located behind the throttles. This ground-stabilised image is automatically connected to the laser ranger, which fires directly at the target and measures the range by calculating the time taken for reflected laser light to return to the aircraft. Keeping the fire committal button pressed will confirm the attack, and, when the continuously computed impact point (CCIP) and target coincide, the weapons will be released automatically. The attack sequence takes place in a matter of seconds, as the Jaguar pilots will try to 'unmask' (reveal their position to the enemy positions around the target) at the last possible moment, leaving themselves with just a few seconds to acquire and line-up on the target.

Terrain masking is vitally important for defence, and the pilot will try to dash in and out of the target area as rapidly as possible before disappearing in the surrounding ground clutter again.

On departure from the target area, reheat can be used to pick up extra speed if necessary, although, as one pilot comments: 'If you select burners, every heat-seeking defensive system in the area will be thinking "yum-yum, there's a nice heat source", so it is not always a good idea, and you have to be careful.' The Adour engines are not immensely powerful, so they are not particularly hot either. This gives the Jaguar a fairly low heat signature, especially when compared with aircraft like the Tornado.

Once it is back in friendly territory, the Jaguar formation can increase its altitude and assume a less warlike flight attitude, not least to avoid the risk of being shot down by friendly forces. Identification friend or foe (IFF) transponders are a vital piece of equipment for sorting the good guys from the bad guys. The flight back to base is normally made at around 360kt, a good speed for low fuel

Below: Each Jaguar squadron has a couple of two-seat dual-control Jaguar T.2As for pilot continuation training. The Jaguar OCU operates a rather larger T.2A fleet, converting No. 4 FTS graduates on to the type.

consumption in most weapon configurations.

On a peacetime return to home base at Coltishall or Lossiemouth the formation will make radio contact with Squadron Operations to give prior notice of its return, for the benefit of the waiting ground crews. Selecting 'Stud Three' will put the formation back into contact with the base air traffic control, and a visual recovery will be made when weather conditions permit. The final arrival over the airfield is made on the tower's radio frequency, with the aircraft positioned in a tight arrow formation. Thirty seconds before arrival in the overhead position the call 'initials' is made. The pilots then begin to break off to port at a height of 1,200ft, making a 4 or 5g turn, deploying airbrakes and moving the throttles back to idle position.

The Jaguar loses speed fairly rapidly, and by the time the aircraft is established on the downwind leg of the airfield circuit the speed has fallen to 260kt. Flaps are now extended to 40°, the airbrakes are brought in, and the speed is down to 230kt. 'Gear down' is selected, and a radio call is made to give the

tower the appropriate intentions (land, overshoot, etc.). The seat and parachute harnesses are tightened and locked, the fuel is checked to ensure that sufficient remains for a safe landing, and the hydraulics are checked, together with the undercarriage 'locked down' lights. Rudder sensitivity is switched from small to large, and full flap is extended before making a 12° AOA turn on to final approach. The engines are set at roughly 93 per cent, and the turn is widened or tightened to take into account the direction and speed of the wind. The 12° AOA is maintained, and a careful check is made that the engines are working correctly, as if one fails at this stage the only real option is for the pilot to eject.

Once the aircraft is established on finals roughly a mile from touchdown, the gear is confirmed down again and the aircraft is positioned on the runway glidepath, usually relying on airfield precision approach path indicators (PAPIs), which should be seen as two red and two white lights, changing to three reds and one white just before landing. The aircraft is aimed to land on the runway

Above: Drab grey/green camouflage is brightened by the dazzling 75th anniversary colours applied to one of No. 41 Squadron's Jaguar GR.1As.

numbers just beyond the 'piano key' markings at the threshold, with a touchdown speed of 140kt. Once it is safely down, the throttles are closed and the aircraft is flared by rotating through 14° or 15° AOA to give a good aerodynamic braking effect. Any greater AOA would probably allow the underfuselage strakes to make contact with the runway. The nose will fall at about 120kt, and then the nosewheel steering can be engaged, with braking commencing below 100kt. A heavy or fast landing can be retarded by releasing the brake parachute, using a handle on the port side of the cockpit.

Having completed its landing roll, the Jaguar is steered clear of the runway and one engine is shut down. A light-weight Jaguar tends to run away with its occupant, and although this would not be a problem with both engines at idle, it does cause the brakes to overheat. The armament switches are 'safed', the ejection seat pins are replaced, the canopy is partly opened and, if the ground marshaller is spotted, the taxying lights are switched off, prompting the marshaller to begin guiding the pilot back into the parking position. A final INS fix is made to establish the system's accuracy, and then the engine is shut down.

After switching off the remaining systems, unstrapping, climbing out and signing the aircraft over to the crew chief (and giving him details of any problems, INS accuracy, fatigue counts and so on), the pilot is free to return to the squadron buildings to begin a careful debriefing of the whole mission. This will establish whether the mission achieved its aims, and what lessons can be learned from it. The formation leader will conduct the debrief, a supervising officer raising appropriate questions as necessary.

The Jaguar does possess one or two vices, notably the two-seat T.2's inability to recover from a spin. The GR.1, as well, can enter a dangerous flat spin from which a pilot cannot eject successfully. It is therefore important to recognise the spin before it develops, and to effect a quick recovery. The aircraft's maximum speed is good, and with afterburners the Jaguar can achieve Mach 1 at low level. Maintenance demands are fairly light, and the Jaguar force can be deployed and returned home without any major unserviceabilities, an achievement which cannot be matched by many other aircraft. The weapons capability is good, too, the RAF aircraft carrying 1,000lb bombs with retarding or free-fall 'slick' tails, and with air-burst, impact or time-delay fuzes. Also carried are laser-guided bombs, CRV-7 air-to-ground rockets (with a speed of Mach 4 and 10lb warheads), two 30mm Aden cannon and CBU-87 or BL.755 cluster bombs, as well as ALQ-101 ECM pods and chaff/flare dispensers.

The Jaguar's overall performance is very good, especially when flown clean, one pilot describing the Jaguar as 'a big Hawk with afterburners'. Normally carrying a hefty fuel and weapon load, it can also carry two AIM-9L Sidewinder air-to-air missiles. This capability was developed for the aircraft during Operation Desert Storm to give it a good self-protection capability. Relying on boresight positioning, the Sidewinder's heat-seeking warhead ensures that any marauding fighter will not 'mix it' with a Jaguar easily. The Jaguar is a quarter of a century old, and a degree of imperfection might be expected. As one pilot says: 'A perfect Jaguar would have a new head-up display, twin fins, a bubble canopy and bigger engines', but it is well respected by its crews, and the RAF's evident reluctance to dispose of its Jaguar fleet is proof enough that the aircraft is more than a match for any other current combat aircraft.

Tornado Tales

Left: A Tornado F.3 with its pilot and navigator, RAF Coningsby.

At the very forefront of the RAF's offensive capability, the Panavia Tornado is numerically the most significant aircraft in the RAF's armoury. Conceived in 1968, the Multi-Role Combat Aircraft (MRCA) was the result of a multinational feasibility study for an aircraft able to fulfil a variety of relatively diverse tasks. Most importantly, the RAF saw in the MRCA the potential for a truly mutli-purpose design which could operate as both a ground-attack/strike platform and a long-range interceptor, able to counter the growing threat posed by Soviet attack aircraft such as the Sukhoi Su-24 and Tupolev Tu-26. The prototype MRCA first flew on 14 August 1974, and the first production-standard interdictor strike (IDS) variant for the RAF made its maiden flight on 10 July 1979. The IDS variant (designated Tornado GR.1 in RAF service) joined the newly-formed Trinational Tornado Training Establishment (TTTE) at RAF Cottesmore on 1 July 1980, marking the beginning of long and distinguished service with the RAF which continues to this day.

The Tornado GR.1, a low-level strike/attack and offensive-support aircraft, effectively replaced the RAF's Avro Vulcan and English Electric Canberra force, as well as RAF Germany's Jaguars and, more recently, the RAF's Hawker Siddeley Buccaneers. Although the GR.1 squadrons no longer exercise their ability to carry nuclear weapons, the RAF's stocks of WE.177 bombs having been withdrawn, the Tornado seems set to remain at the very heart of the RAF's offensive capability. The Tornado squadrons are assigned to Nato, with four squadrons (Nos. 9, 14, 17 and 31) currently located at RAF Bruggen in Germany, although these units

Right: Illustrating the multinational spirit of the TTTE, a trio of Tornado GR.1s display the markings of Britain, Germany and Italy.

will soon return to the UK when RAF Bruggen closes, joining the sole UK-based GR.1 unit, No. 15(R) Squadron, the Tornado Weapons Conversion Unit.

Capable of delivering a wide variety of weapons, the Tornado GR.1 includes conventional 1,000lb high-explosive (HE) bombs in both 'slick' and retarded versions in its primary armament. Laser-guided bombs also form an important part of the Tornado's weapons system, especially now that the thermal imaging and laser designating (TIALD) pod is becoming a more standard part of operations, following its hugely successful (but premature) introduction during Operation Desert Storm. Other weapons options include BL.755 cluster-bomb units, air-launched anti-radar missiles (ALARMs), and the Tornado's unique JP.233 weapons dispenser, employed against airfield targets. Additionally, two Mauser 27mm

cannon are installed in the GR.1's nose and AIM-9L Sidewinder missiles can be carried for self-protection, although the aircraft is also normally equipped with chaff and flare dispensers, electronic countermeasures and radar warning equipment.

Evolved from the basic IDS variant, the Tornado GR.1A is a dedicated reconnaissance aircraft, equipping Nos. 2 and 13 Squadrons at RAF Marham. When the GR.1A first joined the RAF on 3 April 1987 it marked an important milestone in the RAF's reconnaissance capabilities. Gone were the days of clumsy and slow 'wet' film processing; in came a new era of synthetic photography using the GR.1's electro-optical equipment, namely the British Aerospace sideways-looking infra-red (SLIR) and Vinten Linescan 4000 infra-red systems. Recorded video film can be replayed in flight if necessary, and for a truly high-speed result

Above: The TTTE's RAF Tornado GR.1s are gradually emerging from the paint shop with a new overall grey colour scheme which is being progressively applied to the entire RAF Tornado GR.1 fleet.

Above: A 1988 portrait of a Luftwaffe Tornado assigned to the TTTE. Although it is unquestionably a German airframe, the pilot, instructor or both may be RAF personnel, thanks to the 'pooled' nature of Cottesmore's Tornadoes.

the images can be transmitted instantly to an appropriate ground unit, effectively giving ground commanders a real-time eye in the sky. Although the GR.1A has the Mauser cannon removed to make way for the necessary reconnaissance equipment, it remains fully combat-capable in all other respects.

The most recent development of the Tornado IDS to join the RAF's ranks is the GR.1B, a specialised maritime-attack derivative which replaced the RAF's Buccaneer fleet, beginning in 1993. Numbers 12 and 617 Squadrons, based at Lossiemouth in Scotland, are currently assigned to the maritime role, operating a fleet of 24 aircraft equipped to carry the British Aerospace Dynamics (BAeD) Sea Eagle sea-skimming anti-ship missile. Retaining a full combat capability, these GR.1Bs can also carry refuelling pods, giving the squadrons a

'buddy' aerial refuelling capacity and enhancing operational flexibility.

For the immediate future, the Tornado GR.4 will soon enter RAF service, the result of a mid-life upgrade (MLU) programme which will see the Tornado emerge with a new Marconi Defence Systems electronic-warfare suite, an updated weapons control system, an advanced video recording system (with a ground replay facility) and a new computer loading system. The GR.4 will also have a new Ferranti head-up display unit with computer generated symbology, and a Smiths Industries colour cathode-ray tube (CRT) head-down display.

As mentioned previously, the Tornado was also developed into a markedly different aircraft, designed to fulfil the RAF's requirement for a long-range stand-off interceptor to replace both the English Electric Lightning and McDonnell Douglas Phantom.

The result was the Tornado Air Defence Variant (ADV), which entered RAF service on 5 November 1984, the more powerful Tornado F.3 subsequently replacing the F.2 fleet. Unlike the hugely successful IDS variant, the Tornado F.2 and F.3 suffered from a long series of software-system developmental problems, and when the F.2 entered service most of the fleet had concrete ballast in place of radar, which was still being developed. The seemingly endless technical problems surrounding the Tornado ADV's radar and associated equipment attracted a great deal of media interest, and gave the F.3 an undeservedly bad reputation which it retains, to some extent, even today. Undoubtedly the F.3 cannot match the supreme manoeuvrability of Russia's Sukhoi Su-27 or even the USA's

Left: Although Tornadoes would not normally operate with undercarriage extended and wings fully swept, the TTTE, like other Tornado units, regularly practises approaches in this configuration, to simulate a wing-sweep failure.

General Dynamics F-16, but it is often forgotten that the Tornado ADV was never intended to be a 'fighter' in the strictest sense. It was designed to carry stand-off missiles over long ranges, and to have a good loiter capability, in order to protect the UK's huge air-defence region, which stretches over hundreds of miles. It was unfortunate that, by the time the Tornado ADV entered service, the RAF's requirement had largely shifted towards a more traditional 'dogfighter', able to take on the new breed of Russian 'superfighters'.

However, as a pure interceptor the Tornado F.3 has been a major success. With its armament of four BAeD Sky Flash air-to-air missiles – to be replaced by the Hughes AIM-120 advanced medium-range air-to-air missile (AMRAAM) – and four AIM-9L Sidewinders it

can make a rapid transit to a distant Combat Air Patrol (CAP) location and maintain a relatively long patrol, ready to take on beyond-visual-range (BVR) targets. Should enemy aircraft come within visual range the Sidewinders can be employed, and in the unlikely event that a truly close-in fight develops, an IWKA-Mauser 27mm cannon is also fitted. Although the RAF's fighter pilots practise close-in fighting almost daily, the Tornado F.3 is much more likely to seek and destroy its enemy well beyond the range of a visual encounter.

Looking to the future, it is fair to say that the RAF will relinquish the Tornado F.3 at the earliest opportunity. Despite the aircraft's outstanding range and speed performance, the Service is keen to embrace the close-in dogfighting capabilities of the new Eurofighter. As a Tornado navigator explains:

Left: A sunset study of a TTTE Tornado being prepared for engine tests at Cottesmore.

'You want an aeroplane that can detect targets at a long range, looking both up and down and coping with lots of targets simul-taneously. You also need to carry lots of weapons over a long range. The Tornado F.3 does all this very well and meets these criteria in every respect, apart, perhaps, from radar performance. Admittedly it is not as good as the manufacturer initially promised, but having said that it still performs very well indeed. It has a range which is more than adequate and, for example, if I cannot successfully intercept a target after picking it up at around 50 miles, then there is something seriously wrong with me. OK, a supersonic target might need to be detected at around 70 miles, but in that kind of situation the target would probably be fairly high, and a ground radar controller or AWACS [airborne warning and control system] would probably vector me on to it. The Tornado F.3 really is not deficient in any way, despite the reputation it has acquired. It was never designed to be an air-superiority fighter, so I would not want to mix it with a MiG-29 or Su-27, but I would be much happier doing my job in the F.3 than many other aircraft I can think of, especially the Phantom which we used to operate.'

Certainly, the days of quick-reaction alert (QRA) scrambles have almost completely gone, the threat of invading Soviet bombers being little more than a scary memory. Russian 'intruders' are now identified on radar only very infrequently, and normally just a single Tornado will be launched to investigate, largely as a token demonstration of capability rather than a serious attempt to intercept the intruder. For more regular training missions Tornado F.3s will often operate in pairs, flying pre-planned tactics relying on mutual support and cross-cover for both defensive and offensive manoeuvres.

For a typical F.3 sortie, planning begins within the squadron's headquarters at Leuchars (Nos. 43 and 111 Squadrons), Leeming (11 and 25 Squadrons) or Coningsby (5 and 29 Squadrons, together with the F.3

OCU, No. 56[R] Squadron). The pre-flight briefing will include all of the usual information necessary for the sortie, including 'domestics' such as radio frequencies, weather, callsigns and so on. The briefing will then explore the scenario for the mission, the expected (simulated) threat, the position of friendly forces, refuelling support, AWACS assistance, etc. A complete flight plan is then prepared, covering transit routes, turning points, refuelling tanker positions, missile engagement zones and so on, ready for feeding into the aircraft's on-board computers, either directly through the multi-function display (MFD) keyboard in their cockpits or through a programmed cassette which can be loaded into the computer. The information will then be available to the pilots and navigators on their cockpit CRT screens, and suitable information, such as steering commands, can also be repeated on the pilots' HUDs.

Most of the RAF's Tornado F.3 fleet is housed in hardened aircraft shelter (HAS) complexes, and after briefing, planning and kitting-up, the crews take a minibus to their

Below: After completing conversion on to the Tornado, students progress to the Tornado Weapons Conversion Unit. Before moving to Lossiemouth, the TWCU was based at Honington, where this picture was taken in 1990.

respective shelters, where their aircraft are ready for action. After a careful walk-round inspection the crew climbs into the F.3's roomy cockpit to begin a long series of pre-start and pre-taxy switch selections and checks. When they are ready, the twin Rolls-Royce RB.199 Mk.104 turbofans are wound up and the aircraft is ready to emerge from its HAS and begin to taxy towards the active runway. At the runway threshold two aircraft will normally line up line-abreast on either side of the runway centreline. With the checks complete, both pilots will run-up their engines to full 'dry' power and then into 50 per cent afterburner, the Tornado's strong wheelbrakes enabling the aircraft to remain stationary while the wingman waits for a nod from the leader to begin the take-off roll. Then the brakes are released and 80 per cent afterburner is selected, and under a

Right: An unusual view of TWCU Tornadoes on the flight line at Honington, with wings unswept and flaps and slats extended.

combined thrust of over 30,000lb the Tornado accelerates briskly. In just a few seconds it reaches 135kt, at which speed the pilot raises the nose off slightly before gently easing the aircraft into the air at 150kt.

Once they are settled into a departure altitude and direction, the F.3s will assume a transit 'battle' formation, positioned line-abreast with roughly a mile's separation. Larger formations of four or more aircraft will assume a radar trail position on the two lead aircraft, forming a large defensive box. Relatively long transit flights are rare, as most of the RAF's air-defence training is performed over the North Sea, but, even if a lengthy flight is required, the F.3's 'long legs' (it has roughly twice the range of the Phantom which it replaced) enable it to reach a patrol area without refuelling support. Even so, aerial refuelling practice is an important part of operations, and many training missions will include a tanker 'top-up' at some stage. Unlike the Tornado GR.1, which is regularly fitted with a removable 'bolt-on' refuelling probe system, the F.3 has a retractable probe installed in its forward fuselage. To provide a graphic demonstration of the F.3's capabilities, in January 1982 a Tornado ADV prototype flew a demonstration CAP mission from the manufacturer's base at Warton in Lancashire, flying some 375 miles at altitude and then flying a representative CAP pattern at low level for another 2 hours 20 minutes. After returning to Warton the aircraft loitered another 15 minutes before finally touching down, completing a flight of 4 hours 13 minutes with 5 per cent fuel still remaining. Not bad for a gas-guzzling fighter!

Inside the F.3's cockpit, the navigator's instrument panel is dominated by a pair of multi-function CRT display screens which form the core of the aircraft's weapons system (the pilot also has a CRT screen which can repeat information being displayed in the navigator's position). With the Foxhunter radar in 'search' mode, the navigator will begin looking for targets as the pilot steers the aircraft into the appropriate CAP position. Although the 'back-seater' is still referred to as a 'navigator' in the RAF, he or she is responsible for much more than this name implies. Indeed, a great deal of navigation is now routinely performed by the pilot. In effect, the navigator is the equivalent of the United States Air Force's (USAF's) Weapons Systems Operator and the US Navy's Radar Interception Officer merged into one, controlling all of the Tornado's systems other

Above: The TWCU has been renumbered as a reserve squadron and is now No. 15(R) Squadron (formerly an RAFG unit), based at Lossiemouth. The red fin was part of an RAFG flight-safety trial.

Top: No. 31 Squadron is one of Bruggen's four Tornado units, due to relocate to the UK at the end of the century.

Above: A former Vulcan unit, No. 9 Squadron specialises in the use of the BAeD ALARM anti-radiation missile.

than those associated with actually flying the aircraft. The navigator controls the mission while the pilot flies it.

Once established in a CAP pattern, the Tornado pair will separate, each aircraft flying half of a large racetrack pattern aimed in the direction of the anticipated threat. As one pilot flies towards the perceived threat, flying 'up-threat' or 'hot', his wingman will fly the opposite direction, 'down-threat' or 'cold'. On less-common sorties in which just one aircraft flies a CAP, another racetrack pattern will be adopted, positioned broadside to the threat direction so that the crew fly with their backs towards the threat for the least possible amount of time. On other occasions CAPs with a moving datum point might be employed, to keep pace with a naval battle group, for example, while another option is a large figure-of-eight pattern which gives the aircraft a higher cruising speed and more residual momentum for a possible enemy engagement.

Individual radar plots will be displayed on the navigator's screen as short vertical lines with a horizontal crossbar to indicate IFF response. By moving a four-quadrant marker (controlled by joystick) over any of these plots

the navigator can automatically track the target, changing to a 'track-while-scan' mode. The speed, heading and altitude of any target can also be displayed, and one of the two CRT displays will normally be set to a tactical evaluation (Taceval) display, showing a north-oriented view of the whole area surrounding the threat and displaying all available information from AWACS platforms, naval radar or ground controllers, and other fighters. This broad view gives the crew a complete picture of the unfolding scenario, enabling the most appropriate targets to be selected and the most effective action to be taken.

Changing the radar to an attack-display mode, the navigator will select the most suitable weapon at his disposal, probably the Sky Flash missile. The radar will continue to track the target and an aiming dot will appear over it, providing a collision-course steering vector with an allowable steering error (ASE) circle surrounding the dot. The circle's diameter varies according to the missile's operating parameters and the distance to the target. Maximum and minimum launch distances will be displayed and, provided that the aiming dot is surrounded by the ASE circle, a 'hit' is very

likely, if not certain. The Sky Flash has proved to be a very effective missile with good operating reliability, and displayed an excellent 'kill' probability during development trials. It can discriminate between targets flying in close formation, and it will also operate successfully in fairly hostile ECM environments. The only real downside to the missile's performance is that the target must continue to be illuminated until impact, and this could obviously cause the target to get uncomfortably close to the Tornado. However, the prospect of 'fire-and-forget' missiles means that even this disadvantage will soon be eliminated.

If the interceptor and target aircraft should close to within visual range of each other, the prospect of a close-in dogfight becomes a reality. There is no doubt that the Tornado F.3 is not a 'fighter', and was it never meant to be one, but the new generation of highly manoeuvrable fighters operated by both East and West, and a complete change in world affairs, means that the F.3 is much more likely than ever before to encounter fighters in close-in combat. Although it was designed to intercept long-range Soviet bombers, the Tornado might well be required to 'turn and burn' with the best fighters in the business,

Above: Co-located with No. 13 Squadron at Marham, No. 2 Squadron – or, to be more precise, No. II(AC) Squadron – is assigned to tactical reconnaissance, with a secondary offensive-support mission. This picture shows to advantage the Tornado's thrust-reverser buckets.

Above: Like the aircraft of No. 2 Squadron, No. 13 Squadron's Tornado GR.1As are equipped with sophisticated reconnaissance equipment which provides the RAF with real-time, high-resolution synthetic imagery.

Right: Like many front-line RAF aircraft, most Tornados are housed in HASs clustered around the RAF's bases.

target area, while staff in the operations cabin decide which pilot will lead the mission and who his wingmen will be, based upon their information on aircraft status, and which pilots are available, etc.

When they have completed their mission and returned to their dispersed site, the Harriers will be quickly towed back into their camouflaged hides. The pilots then reconnect their cable links (plugged into the fuselage by the ground crew) with the operations cabin to begin an 'in-brief', which includes a mission report ('MisRep') from each pilot, outlining their individual performances in terms of target acquisition, damage assessment, aircraft serviceability, mission timings and so on. This information is then rapidly passed to the central tasking agency so that additional attacks, reconnaissance flights or new targets can be tasked as appropriate.

So how does the Harrier pilot fly his mission? After receiving his ATM from the

operations cabin, he will check that the required TOT is achievable and that there is sufficient time to plan, brief and fly the sortie. The flight leader will then allocate specific tasks to each of his wingmen. For example, one pilot will be responsible for calculating the Harrier's vertical or short take-off and landing (VSTOL) performance figures for the sortie, while another will be responsible for gathering predicted weather data for the target area and route, although the Harriers (being dedicated CAS aircraft) are likely to be deployed close to the active battlefield area, making the route to and from the target relatively short. The pilot will then locate the target on his Ordnance Survey map, be it a bridge, a troop concentration, a command building, a petrol, oil and lubricants (POL) site, or whatever else may have been tasked. He will decide what weapons should be used to destroy the target, although, as mentioned, this matter may be decided by the tasking

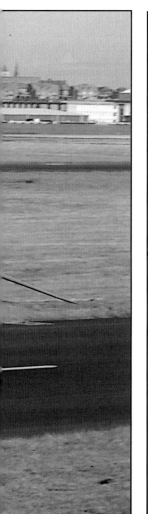

Below right: A nostalgic view of a Harrier GR.3 flown by the OC No. 4 Squadron, complete with his 'special' squadron colours on its tail, as it hooks up to a VC10 tanker.

authority, who may have made their own plans to match targets with appropriate weapons. Even so, the pilots may change the plan. For example, there would be little point in attacking a bridge with a cluster-bomb unit, as this weapon is designed to disable armoured vehicles and troops rather than destroy concrete. In this case a standard 1,000lb bomb would be much more effective. Conversely, a 1,000lb bomb would not cause much damage to armoured vehicles spread over a relatively wide area, so the right weapons have to be chosen carefully.

The next task is to establish an attack path on to the target. For something like a bridge it would be foolish to attempt a bombing run from an offset angle of 90°, as it would be very easy to straddle the target with bombs without actually hitting it. Attacking longitudinally would also be ineffective if the left or right positioning was less than accurate. The optimum attack for this target would be a 30° or 45° oblique approach, ensuring the best chance of a direct hit. Another important consideration with regard to the

approach path is the 'unmask' point, at which the aircraft will emerge from the surrounding terrain to enable the pilot to see his target. Unmasking too late leaves the pilot insufficient time to locate the target, but unmasking too early gives the target's defenders plenty of time to track the incoming Harrier and bring anti-aircraft defences to bear. So there has to be a balance between keeping the aircraft hidden and the need to locate the target visually. On average, the Harrier pilot will try to keep the unmasked final approach to the target down to approximately 10 seconds. To ensure that the aircraft is positioned in precisely the right place just a few seconds before weapons release, the route to the target must be planned with great precision, making use of various lead-in visual features to correct the path constantly en route.

Harriers rarely fly solo, and most missions will involve at least two aircraft, with four aircraft being a typical 'package'. En route to the target, and on the return leg, the aircraft will assume a 'battle' formation, separated by

Above: The Harrier T.2, later modified to T.4 standard, was the dual-control variant of the GR.1/GR.3. A couple were usually operated by each of the Harrier squadrons. The Harrier OCU operated a large fleet of two-seaters, represented here by this T.4 of No. 20(R) Squadron, the shadow designation now applied to what was No. 233 OCU.

relatively wide distances of perhaps two miles or even more, if terrain and visibility permit. A close formation would present enemy defences with a good target, so wide separation is a useful tactic, although care has to be taken to ensure that each pilot does not lose sight of the lead aircraft. Additionally, this loose formation enables pilots to watch each other's six o'clock, the most vulnerable position and the direction from which enemy interceptors are likely to mount an attack.

As part of the mission's defensive tactics, the leader's wingman may well elect to approach the target from a different direction from that chosen by the flight leader, possibly cutting-in on the leader's approach route just a few seconds before bomb release. However, a 1,000lb bomb will create a significant amount of debris and a huge cloud of smoke, through which any wingman certainly would not want to fly. Consequently a 'slash' attack is a useful option, the wingman making his approach at 45° to the first attack, some 20 or 30 seconds after the

leader. This means that although the Harriers will operate as a combined package of two or four aircraft, each pilot must prepare his own individual attack route, to coincide with the leader.

When planning the route, the location of lead-in features is a very important consideration, and the most prominent and easily recognisable locations are always chosen. In the UK and Germany it is fairly easy to find a lake, wood, motorway junction or something equally conspicuous, and by locating these features the pilot can then use conventional navigation techniques to bring the aircraft on to the target. In a Harrier GR.3 (now withdrawn from RAF service), the pilot would fly over his selected lead-in feature, start a stopwatch and fly the aircraft at a steady 480kt on the required heading. After a predetermined number of seconds the Harrier would then arrive at the target point. With the advent of the new-generation Harrier GR.7, the pilot's task is made somewhat easier. He simply calculates in advance the latitude and longitude coordinates of the target, and these can then be fed directly into the Harrier's on-board computer, giving the pilot a precise bearing and range to the target. When the pilot overflies the selected IP he hits the waypoint overfly (WOF) switch, and the Harrier's computer switches the pilot's HUD into air-to-ground readout mode. The computer also checks the aircraft's radio altimeter to calculate the height of the target, and the system will then give the pilot a precise lead-in to the target, via his HUD screen.

A typical day of operations 'in the field' in Germany begins at 0530Z ('Zulu' being GMT), normally equating to 0730 local time in Germany. After getting out of bed, shaving, eating, etc., the pilots gather together their sleeping kit, ready to move to a new dispersal site. After collecting his flying helmet, each

Right: The RAF's
most recent combat
aircraft acquisition is
the dual-control
Harrier T.10, seen
here in the markings
of No. 20(R)
Squadron, RAF
Wittering.

pilot walks to his aircraft, pausing to sign an
'aircraft turnaround' certificate attached to
the individual aircraft's Form 700 book. This
enables the pilot to endorse what would
otherwise be a lengthy list of separate boxes
(he takes the Form 700 book with him, ready
to move on with the aircraft). Following a
quick but careful check of the aircraft's
exterior, the pilot climbs into the Harrier's
cockpit and begins what could be a long
stay, awaiting the call to initiate a mission.
Until that happens, the pilot remains on alert
inside the cockpit, leaving only occasionally to
answer the usual calls of nature.

Attaching oneself to a Harrier GR.7 is much
simpler than in the earlier Harrier GR.3, simply
because the redesigned cockpit is much
larger. The aircraft's computer navigation
system can be aligned before strapping-in if
necessary, as AC power can be supplied by
an internal gas-turbine starter unit. Once
inside the cockpit the pilot attaches the leg
restraints, personal survival pack (PSP;
comprising dinghy, flares, etc.) and personal
equipment connector (PEC; oxygen, communications and air for the anti-g suit) before
routeing the various harness straps into the
quick-release box (QRB). When this task is

completed, the communications equipment
is switched on and the fuel pumps are
selected, together with the electronic fuel
control system (a manual system also being
checked at the same time). Working through
the switches from the left to the right of the
cockpit, other items are also selected such as
autostabilisers, undercarriage down, flaps up,
left-hand TV screen showing the built-in test
(BIT) list, and the chaff/flare dispensers, before
moving to the Harrier's unique nozzle vector
lever.

Next come the basic flight instruments and
the WOF switch, the CCIP switch, the Tacan
equipment and the appropriate altitude base
height, below which the aircraft's instrumen-
tation will automatically provide visual and
audible warnings. The IFF frequency is
chosen, and the weapons selection (WPS) is
checked, enabling the pilot to programme his
weapons release sequence on the options
display unit. The HUD's brightness is adjusted
and a back-up aiming sight can be selected
should the main system fail. Below this are
the main instruments such as the altimeter,
attitude indicator, airspeed indicator, vertical
speed indicator, angle-of-attack indicator and
turn-and-slip indicator.

Above: A head-on view of a Harrier GR.5 with its refuelling probe extended. The GR.5 was the early version of the new-generation Harrier developed by McDonnell Douglas and British Aerospace, and the GR.5 airframes were quickly brought up to the latest GR.7 standard.

Between the pilot's knees, low on the instrument panel, is the sensor control panel for the TV and laser tracker mounted in the Harrier's nose, together with the alignment knob for the inertial navigation platform and video recording switch, plus a few circuit breakers. Up on the right-hand side is the engine data panel, which shows the engine revolutions, the jet-pipe temperature (JPT) and duct pressure to the reaction-control nozzles, as well as fuel flow and tailplane position. Further to the right is the engine nozzle position indicator, and below this is the moving-map display, with options for different scales depending on whether a sortie is being flown at high, medium or low level. To the right of this is an ECM panel featuring Zeus, an on-board electronic warfare (EW) suite recognised as being one of the best pieces of EW equipment currently available. Below this is a fuel panel. On the right-hand console there are various caution lights for systems such as brake pressure, hydraulic pressure and cabin pressure. Further to the right are switches for the auxiliary power unit (APU), the standby radio and the auxiliary communications and navigation identification panel (ACNIP), a

back-up system for the up-front controller (UFC). Also on this side of the cockpit are controls for the internal lighting, which in the Harrier GR.7 is all-green, including the warning lights.

Having completed the left-to-right switch selections the pilot can begin the engine start-up sequence, and after removing the safety pins for the ejection seat and miniature detonating cord (MDC), he signals to the ground crew to remove the engine air intake blanking plates. Once start clearance is obtained, the low-pressure (LP) fuel cock is turned on, the electronic fuel control master switch is turned on, the high-pressure (HP) fuel cock is switched off, the manual fuel system is switched off and the booster pumps are switched on. The starting switch, located on the electrical panel near the APU switch, is then selected. At this stage the APU runs down initially, reverting to DC power if required, to maintain supply to the on-board systems before the engine is engaged, at which stage the APU winds up again. As the engine starts, the fuel HP cock is opened, initiating the rest of the starting procedure, while the pilot checks the JPT. If the temperature rises too rapidly, causing a 'hot start' (too much fuel being injected into the engine), the throttle is closed slightly. Throughout this 'hot' procedure the pilot keeps an eye on the ground crew for any indication that an engine fire might have erupted. Likewise, the engine nozzles are set to the aft position to prevent hot air being ingested by the engine and exacerbating the problem.

With the engine running smoothly, the post-start checks are completed and the Harrier is ready to taxy to the runway or prepared take-off clearing. The engine nozzles are checked to ensure that they are functioning properly, and are then set at 10° to avoid damaging the tail surfaces. Even so, the jet efflux flowing over the tailplane can be felt by the pilot through the control column as the aircraft taxies, with a brief pause to check brake function.

With the canopy closed and the aircraft positioned on the runway, a solo, pair or stream take-off run can be commenced, depending on tactics, wind conditions and the size of the runway. Taking off in the Harrier is a unique experience, either vertically or conventionally. Harriers seldom take off vertically for operational missions, as a fully fuelled aircraft would not be capable of carrying much ordnance if everything were to be hauled straight into the air purely on engine power. A more conventional short take-off run is usually employed, enabling the Harrier to achieve some forward airspeed and lift before the engine nozzles are rotated to punch the aircraft up from the runway. Because of the aircraft's purposely designed lightweight airframe (to enable the Rolls-Royce Pegasus engine to lift it), the initial rate of acceleration on take-off is very impressive, and greater than that of many contemporary aircraft which have the luxury of afterburners. At light take-off weights the Harrier becomes airborne in less than 200ft. The drag factor does eventually overcome thrust as speed increases, but the Harrier possesses some outstanding low-speed handling qualities. Take-off speed is predetermined by aircraft weight and ambient air temperature. Likewise, the speed at which the nozzles are lowered to 50° to push the aircraft into the air is also calculated in advance.

The Harrier's fuel-control system is fairly complicated, as great emphasis has to be placed upon engine reliability. An aircraft which hovers on jet thrust requires almost

Right: A brace of Harrier GR.7s from No. 20(R) Squadron, wearing the latest low-visibility grey camouflage being applied progressively to the whole Harrier fleet.

instant engine response, which in turn requires a sophisticated means of supplying the engine with fuel. To check the system before take-off the throttle is deliberately 'slammed' from idle to 55 per cent and then held while the time taken to achieve the increased thrust is established. It should take 5 seconds or less. Increasing power to full thrust would cause the aircraft's tyres to slip on their mountings, although the brakes would hold. After returning the throttle to idle, the nozzles are checked for rotation to 50° and the engine duct pressure is checked. Finally, the inlet guide vanes (IGVs) are checked. These are designed to move in flight to maintain air pressure across the LP intake stage of the engine.

After a final look to confirm that the ejection-seat safety pins are stowed in their flight positions, the pilot quickly glances at the fuel and flap settings, and the master arm safety switch, before obtaining take-off clearance. Little verbal communication is necessary, and for a two- or four-ship departure hand signals suffice, with a deliberate nod to start the take-off roll, another nod to initiate short take-off ('STO') and another to raise the gear (these signals

obviously apply to a pairs formation). After running-up to full power, the brakes are released and the Harrier surges forward, rumbling over the runway surface (which could be a fairly basic semi-prepared strip) and sometimes giving the pilot a fairly rough ride. A few seconds later the take-off speed (normally around 120kt) is reached and the aircraft enters a 12° AOA climb, making a fairly steep departure to avoid trees or other obstructions surrounding the area.

On particularly hot days in Germany some take-off runs are made with less than a full fuel load, to enable the Harrier to achieve a short take-off within safety limits. However, the Harrier's range does not necessarily have to be compromised by fuel load, as the GR.7 has an in-flight refuelling probe which gives the aircraft almost unlimited endurance, depending upon tanker support. Full thrust is not normally employed for take-off during peacetime training, in order to extend engine life, but, if full power is required, water injection can be used, cooling the rear portion of the Pegasus to increase revolutions by 6 or 7 per cent and provide a corresponding 1,000 or 1,500lb of thrust. However, the 50gal of water will last

Below: A Harrier GR.7, the latest variant of the remarkable VTOL fighter/bomber, proudly displays the markings of No. 1 Squadron. Assigned to offensive support (ground-attack) duties, the RAF's GR.7s are now fully capable of performing night attacks, thanks to the aircraft's sophisticated infra-red sensor system and the pilot's NVGs.

only 80 seconds, and if 10gal are used for take-off only a minute's reserve will remain. Consequently the pilot must be careful to identify and locate his dispersed landing site after completing the mission, as his 'hover time' will be severely limited at heavy weights if his water reserve is already depleted.

During the take-off procedure a check that the water injection is flowing will be followed by a look at the engine rpm. This is a vital check if water is being used, as some of the Harrier's take-off areas can be very small, and if the water-injection system fails the engine will not develop full power, and the pilot will have to make an instant decision as to whether to abort the take-off or continue. In a confined space and with rapid acceleration there is virtually no time to think, and if the water-injection system did fail in such a situation the pilot would probably have no choice but to eject. Flap settings vary according to the take-off, 'cruise' (up), 'auto' (between 5° and 25°) and 'STOL' (full deflection for short take-off and landing) being the options. During a normal pairs take-off the flaps are set at 'auto'; full deflection causes the Harrier to bounce into the air quite noticeably, making close formation flying fairly tricky. On a dispersed site, however, STOL flap is almost always used, and once the aircraft is safely airborne the undercarriage is quickly retracted. As already mentioned, radio communications are always relatively brief as a matter of routine, and they are kept to an absolute minimum during an exercise or operational mission.

On a typical sortie the outbound 'chatter' is likely to be as follows:

'Bottle formation is airborne, Stud Eight.' (Harrier pilot announcing his take-off and radio frequency.)

'Roger, Bottle formation, cleared to Stud Eight.' (Control tower or local controller, confirming.)

'Stud Eight, go.' (Harrier pilot switching radio.)

'Bottle one,' 'two,' 'three,' 'four'. (Each Harrier pilot checking in.)

'Bottle four aircraft departing, VFR, one thousand feet.' (Harrier flight leader leaving the local area at a height of 1,000ft under visual flight rules, i.e. out of cloud or bad weather.)

'Roger, no known traffic in the area, QNH is nine-eight-five, you are cleared en route, good day, Stud Fifteen.' (Tower confirming local altimeter setting.)

'Bottle two,' 'three,' 'four'. (Harrier pilots changing to the next radio frequency.)

The aircraft will then transit from the launch area at around 1,000ft, avoiding flying any lower to minimise disturbance to the local population. Indeed, flights over Germany can no longer be flown at the usual low-level altitude of 250ft, owing to new government rules. Consequently many Harrier flights are now routed to the UK to take advantage of the more relaxed height restrictions. However, even in the UK routes are always planned to avoid built-up, populated areas and other isolated sites such as hospitals. As a result, the uninhabited areas of Scotland and Wales are often the best areas for flying fairly realistic training missions at 250ft. The numerous avoidance areas certainly make flight planning more difficult, but they are often treated as simulated missile or AAA sites which would have to be avoided in any case, and are thus

Above: Three Harrier GR.5s in the markings of No. 233 OCU, shortly after the type was introduced into RAF service.

used constructively as part of the training process.

Normally flying in battle formation, the Harriers will position themselves as a pair (or two pairs) line-abreast, separated by 2,000–3,000 yards. The separation distance is kept as wide as possible for tactical purposes, and sometimes the task of maintaining visual contact with the leader can be quite difficult, the Harrier becoming little more than a dot on the horizon and often disappearing into ground clutter. In a four-ship formation the second pair will fly in trail position, roughly 30 seconds behind the leader and sometimes (for tactical reasons) displaced laterally.

Once they are clear of populated areas the aircraft will descend to low level and begin the business of 'contour-hugging' their way around their chosen route. In the UK the need to avoid countless noise-sensitive areas

tends to channel low-level flights into fairly predictable routes, and turning points are often used repeatedly, simply because they have to be instantly recognised as the pilot dashes over the area at 480kt. It is not uncommon for distinctive buildings such as power stations to be used in this fashion almost daily.

Thundering in towards the target at 480kt (over 500mph), the Harrier handles well, although the ride at low level (250ft in peacetime, but lower in an operational environment) is not exactly smooth. In typical European conditions the pilot can expect a variety of sunshine, rain, cloud, fog or even snow and hail, all of which affect the aircraft's handling. In particularly turbulent conditions the high-speed, low-level approach to the target can be pretty exciting, particularly when the pilot is busy looking for the target and trying to avoid enemy defences. Once the WOF switch has been selected, the pilot checks that the armament master switches are selected 'on' and, having already selected the appropriate weapons release sequence, he is ready to turn his attention back to the HUD, on to which a green diamond symbol is being generated. This is the computer's predicted target position, and the pilot can confidently expect the target to appear inside the diamond once the aircraft has flown along the approach route. However, the RAF accepts that computers are not infallible (they also have an annoying habit of 'crashing' when you least want them to), so traditional stopwatch-and-calculation navigation techniques are still used, to ensure that the attack will still succeed if the computer does make a mistake.

Assuming that the system is working properly, the pilot can also select a television camera housed in the Harrier's nose, which will give between six and seven times magnification to show in much greater detail where the computer is targeted. If another switch is selected the camera will track the target, enabling the computer to fine-tune the accuracy of its weapon delivery. On this CCIP attack a cross will appear on the HUD, predicting where the bombs will impact on the target, provided the pilot presses the 'pickle' button on his control column. The bombs can also be dropped automatically by selecting 'Auto' mode. The pilot still presses his pickle button, but does so slightly ahead of the target, and the computer will then decide the precise moment at which to release the weapons.

Although the Harrier's computerised bombing system appears to make the task of weapons delivery simple, it must be remembered that the pilot is flying at 480kt at 250ft or less, towards what would probably be a

heavily defended target. Under such circumstances it is very difficult to devote much attention to a television screen or a computer display, when just a second of distraction could be sufficient for the aircraft to hit the ground. If the HUD diamond symbol appears to the left or right of the actual target position, the pilot slews the diamond on to the target visually, by physically flying the aircraft into position before locking-on to an automatic attack. However, the heavy workload tends to preclude the use of 'TV attacks' as a primary means of delivering weapons. The television system is much more practical for medium-altitude attacks, even though the RAF has long believed that anything other than a low-level attack would be suicidal.

This situation changed quite dramatically following experience gained during the 1991 Gulf War, when air supremacy was achieved

Below: A close-up of the GR.5, illustrating the bolt-on but retractable refuelling probe and the weapons stations under the port wing, complete with a self-protection Sidewinder AAM.

over Iraq, enabling most attacks to be made from the relative safety of about 10,000ft, an altitude for which the Harrier's computer and TV system would be ideally suited. However, the RAF recognises that the Gulf War situation does not necessarily apply to any other theatres of operation, where aerial supremacy might not be achievable, so its fast-jet pilots still place a great emphasis on low-level capability.

Forward Air Controllers (FACs) work regularly with the Harrier force. The GR.7's excellent laser system can detect even the smallest amount of laser energy being reflected from a target and display its position and range very accurately on the cockpit display, enabling the pilot to switch to an Auto attack if necessary. In operational exercises FACs will often operate covertly, using hand-held laser designators to illuminate targets which can quickly be picked off by the Harrier force. Typical CAS attacks often require the use of CBUs to disable armour or personnel, and for a CBU attack an over-the-target height of 100ft is normally chosen, rising to 150ft for conventional 1,000lb bombs. The approach speed is usually 480kt or sometimes faster, depending on the tactical situation and the type of attack. The RAF's Harriers have also readopted the Matra SNEB rocket-launcher pod, originally used on the Harrier GR.1, and the AIM-9L Sidewinder air-to-air missile (AAM) can also be carried, giving the Harrier a very respectable self-defence capability.

With its unique performance characteristics the Harrier is able to 'mix it' with fighters if necessary, the capability to 'viff' (vector in forward flight; move the engine nozzles forward to increase turning performance sharply) being particularly valuable if a high-performance fighter is on the Harrier's tail. This manoeuvre is useful at the top of a loop, where the Harrier can be pitched into the

vertical almost instantaneously by swivelling the nozzles to the 40° position. Likewise, turning the nozzles to the braking stop position while descending vertically will stabilise the aircraft's speed at around 150kt, and even an Su-27 or a MiG-29 is going to have a hard time bringing a missile or gun to bear in that kind of manoeuvre. Likewise, even in the horizontal plane a Harrier can be quickly pushed into a correct missile firing position by 'viffing' it on to the target. Harrier pilots are also well versed in the art of 'dropping one's knickers', a term used to describe the dropping of a parachute retarded 1,000lb bomb in an enemy fighter's face, an easy way seriously to upset even the most determined enemy fighter ace.

During its return to base, or to a new dispersed site, the Harrier formation will remain at low level if necessary or climb to medium altitude for a more relaxed transit. On many missions the Harrier's aerial refuelling capability will be practised and a hook-up with a tanker will be arranged, usually in one of the refuelling 'boxes' over the North Sea. Once back in the local airfield area, the aircraft will descend to make a close-echelon formation approach over the airfield at 1,500ft, running in at 480kt before breaking left to turn on to individual landing circuits.

Once it is in the circuit the Harrier is flown on AOA settings rather than speed, and conventional forward-flight landings can always be made at 140–150kt. However, with a low fuel load and weapons dropped, the lightweight Harrier is more likely to be landed vertically, either as part of an operational approach to a field site or as the culmination of a training exercise. With the engine nozzles brought fully forward, the aircraft's forward airspeed quickly decays to zero and suddenly the conventional feel of a manoeuvrable combat aircraft is replaced by the unique sensations of the Harrier, the pilot being perched on top of a column of jet thrust. Having first noted the local wind speed and direction, the pilot always flies into wind as the aircraft decelerates, keeping very conscious of crosswind conditions, which have an increasing effect upon the aircraft as it slows down to the hover.

During the transition from about 90kt to 30kt the Harrier can produce yaw-induced intake drag, which can kill if the pilot is unaware of it. The wing will produce some lift, but if one wing produces more lift than the other the effect of a crosswind in the huge air intakes will induce a yawing movement which, if it is combined with the asymmetric wing lift, will cause the aircraft to roll and flip over with disastrous results. The AOA is therefore kept low and the slow transition to the hover is performed with great care, as the pilot lines up with the runway or looks for visual references to locate a dispersed landing site.

Stabilising at 50ft in landing configuration with flaps and landing gear down, the aircraft will hover comfortably, control being achieved through the puffer ducts located in the wingtips, nose and tail. These bleed jet thrust from the engine and function in the same way as the conventional flying controls, responding directly to inputs from the control column and providing greater or lesser airflow to achieve movement. Although the hover is stable, the sensation in the cockpit is still very unusual, the huge amount of static thrust causing the aircraft to shake quite noticeably. Likewise, engine fumes creep into the cockpit, and when combined with the increased noise level (with no forward speed to effectively 'blow away' the noise, as in conventional aircraft), this certainly makes the hover very exciting, even for the most experienced pilot.

Once the pilot is satisfied that a safe landing can be made in the correct position, the engine thrust is slightly reduced to begin a gentle descent. In a matter of seconds the Harrier is gently deposited back on the ground, and is quickly taxied back to the flight line or dispersed 'hide'. After shutting down the engine, various post-flight checks are completed before the pilot returns the Form 700 to the ground crew with details of how long the aircraft has been airborne, what faults have developed and how much fuel has been used. Airframe and engine fatigue data are also monitored, and the types of take-off and landings used, together with details of the weapons carried and/or dropped. All of these details are useful in building a complete picture of the airframe's fatigue state.

The Harrier GR.7 is a fairly robust aircraft, however, and it can withstand rigorous applications of positive and negative g. The only really serious airframe hazard is a birdstrike. The engine is also robust, and performs remarkably well, the only possible criticism being that more thrust would be an advantage if it were available. Rolls-Royce is actively promoting a more powerful Pegasus engine for the Harrier, and both the RAF and USMC may well purchase this powerplant during the life cycle of the GR.7, which is likely to remain in RAF service beyond 2010. The Pegasus is a reliable engine which relights easily if a flame-out occurs, and the Harrier is a reliable aircraft with a good serviceability rate.

Perhaps the only potential problem is a generator failure, which, on an 'electric jet' such as the Harrier GR.7, with many systems relying on electrical power, is a difficulty if the situation arises. But in overall terms the Harrier has few vices, being a truly unique aircraft and the world's only VTOL-capable warplane. The navigation and weapons systems are first class, and only all-out speed is inferior to other CAS aircraft. A two-man cockpit might possibly be an advantage, as the pilot's workload is certainly extremely high. Even a very confident Harrier pilot would admit that a second pair of eyes and hands would always be an advantage, but the Harrier's abilities outshine any disadvantages. The capability to operate from virtually any location makes the Harrier a vital asset for the modern RAF.

More recently, the Harrier GR.7 has acquired a night-attack capability through the introduction of night-vision goggles (NVGs) for its pilots. The cover of darkness has always been an important part of military operations, used by forces to reposition troops and equipment. This is borne out by the fact that more than half of the former Soviet Army's training was geared towards night operations, in response to the West's superior daytime intelligence gathering systems. Night attack is not a new tactic, but it is becoming an increasingly important part of the RAF's operations.

Because of the development of defensive systems, night attack was not a major part of the RAF's post-Second World War operations. Only with the advent of the Tornado GR.1 and its automatic low-level terrain-following radar did the RAF seriously re-enter the night-flying business. By comparison, the Harrier was designed as a daytime attack aircraft, and was introduced to the night-flying role during the 1990s. This followed the completion of a development programme at the Royal Aircraft Establishment, Farnborough, where a Harrier and Buccaneer were used in part of the 'Nightbird' programme, designed to develop a combined system of NVGs and forward-looking infra-red (FLIR) for the Harrier fleet. The programme was very successful, and the first representative night-attack sortie was flown by a Harrier on 11 December 1990.

The NVG system works by amplifying the available light from the moon, stars and 'cultural lighting' (the RAF's term for street lights, etc.) to a level at which the pilot can confidently operate the aircraft as if he were flying in daylight conditions. The Harrier's cockpit lighting had to be modified so that it was compatible with the NVG system, otherwise the goggles would also amplify the internal lights, causing a 'blooming' effect similar to being blinded by oncoming headlights on a night-time road. Naturally, the goggles do not give the pilot perfect all-round vision, but with a 40° field of view the effect is rather like looking through a pair of toilet-roll tubes held against the eyes.

Below: The Harrier's unique thrust-vectoring nozzles are clearly visible in this study, indicating that the aircraft is flying partly on jet lift as the pilot brings it round on to the runway with its landing gear extended.

The goggles are attached to the pilot's flying helmet, and can be swivelled aside when not in use. Because they are attached to the helmet they will obviously move wherever the pilot turns his head, and with good night conditions (no cloud and a full moon) the resulting picture is almost as good as daylight. However, the effect does deteriorate in poorer weather. The only small disadvantage to the NVG system is that the goggles add some weight to the helmet, but for safety reasons they are designed to separate from the helmet if the ejection-seat handle is pulled, as the additional weight of the goggles would cause serious neck injuries to any pilot who tried to eject with them still fitted. In many ways the system is much better than the USMC equivalent, their AV-8B-compatible goggles being separate units which are stored in the cockpit for take-off and landing.

The FLIR system fitted to the Harrier GR.7 operates in the far infra-red band. It is designed to detect the heat emitted by objects or surfaces, and is totally unaffected by ambient light (i.e. it will operate in total darkness). All objects give off an infra-red signature, and the system can easily detect target objects such as buildings, bridges or armoured vehicles. The infra-red sensor assembles the incoming information into a picture which is fed into the Harrier's HUD or on to one of the head-down display (HDD) TV screens. The resulting image gives approximately 20° field of view, presented at eye level on the HUD and mixed with the usual HUD symbology for the aircraft and weapons systems. Unusually, the green image can be displayed as white-hot (like a photographic negative) or black-hot, the change in polarity sometimes producing a clearer image, depending upon prevailing conditions.

Also incorporated in the FLIR system is a capacity for identifying thermal targets, which can be displayed on the HUD with a series of inverted arrows which point at each object. Thus the Harrier pilot can literally have his targets pointed out to him. The whole FLIR system can be controlled through the Harrier's HOTAS systems, which means that selections can be made without the pilot having to remove his hands from the control column and throttle – a superb piece of design which makes the pilot's tasks much easier.

As might be expected, the introduction of this night-attack capability has revolutionised the RAF's Harrier operations. Air bases which appear to have ceased operations, with all airfield lighting deceptively switched off, can still be very active, with Harrier operations (including ground preparations) taking place in total darkness and radio silence, only the inevitable sound of engine noise signifying that activity is taking place. This capability could be used to great advantage for dispersed operations in a wartime environment. For peacetime flying, however, the RAF has to try to reconcile the Harrier's new capabilities with the practicalities of day-to-day life. Night flying is generally restricted to approximately 2300, and during the summer this obviously restricts the time in which night flying can realistically take place. But the Harrier's new capabilities have given the RAF what amounts to virtually a new aeroplane, when compared with the first-generation Harrier GR.1 and GR.3. The aircraft can operate in the CAS role, flying against targets just ahead of allied troop lines, or as a battlefield air interdictor, flying sorties much further into enemy territory and destroying support services and structures. With a better payload and range capability than the Jaguar, the Harrier GR.7 is virtually on a par with the Tornado GR.1 in terms of overall capability, and looks set to remain a vital part of the RAF's offensive capability for at least another ten years, and possibly much longer.

Right: The majestic BAe VC10, in the shape of a C.1K of No. 10 Squadron. Although by no means a modern aircraft, the VC10 still provides the RAF with a high-speed strategic transport capability.

Right: Following the Falklands conflict, former airline Lockheed TriStars were acquired by the RAF and converted to a dual tanker/ transport role, effectively increasing the RAF's global transport capability.

Left: A TriStar from No. 216 Squadron on Brize Norton's huge 10,000ft runway.

Right: Demonstrating the TriStar's refuelling capability, a gaggle of No. 74 Squadron F-4J Phantoms top-up over the North Sea.

Left: Customers queue for a fuel top-up. A TriStar tanker/transport formates with a VC10K tanker and a VC10 C.1 transport, joined by a pair of Buccaneers and a pair of Fleet Air Arm Sea Harriers.

Right: The unusual sight of all three refuelling hoses trailing from a VC10 tanker.

Left: Representing Brize Norton's transport fleet, a No. 216 Squadron TriStar leads a VC10 C.1K tanker/transport of No. 10 Squadron (left) and a VC10 K.2 of No. 101 Squadron (right).

Left: The TriStar and VC10 together. The strategic transport VC10s operated by No. 10 Squadron have now all been converted to the dual tanker/transport role, with refuelling pods fitted under the outer wings.

Below: The VC10 can deliver fuel to every RAF aircraft type fitted with a refuelling probe. All of the Nimrod ASW fleet are probe-equipped, as demonstrated by this hook-up over the North Sea.

Right: Having played a vital part in the RAF's Gulf War operations, a VC10 of No. 101 Squadron returns to the UK, complete with appropriate nose artwork: 'The Empire Strikes Back'.

Right: The VC10s of No. 101 Squadron are of two versions: the short-fuselaged K.2, seen here, and the longer-fuselaged K.3.

Left: Supporting RAF fighter operations is a major part of No. 101 Squadron's activities. Here a VC10 K.3 refuels two Tornado F.3s from No. 11 Squadron during a CAP mission from Leeming.

Left: RAF Tornado fighters take on fuel from the VC10's wing-mounted hoses. The centreline hose, which has a greater fuel delivery rate, is reserved for larger customers such as the Nimrod.

Left: The graceful lines of the Handley Page Victor, shortly before the type was retired. For many years the standard RAF tanker aircraft, these former nuclear bombers were operated by Nos. 55 and 57 Squadrons, based at Marham.

Right: Three Victors together for the last time, the lead aircraft carrying nose artwork applied during the Gulf War.

Right: The Victor force was heavily committed to RAF Gulf operations. Here a K.2 is seen at Muharraq, among Bahrain International Airport's hangars.

Below: Back on the runway at Marham, a Victor K.2 displays its unmistakable profile, framed by its huge brake parachute.

Above: The Hawker Siddeley Argosy is often regarded as a fairly unremarkable aircraft, but history records that the 'Whistling Wheelbarrow' served the RAF with great distinction throughout the 1960s, making long-range transport flights to countless RAF outposts around the world. The last surviving RAF examples were relegated to ground-training duties at Cosford.

Below: Following the demise of the Argosy fleet, the RAF adopted the Lockheed C-130 Hercules for tactical transport duties. More than 25 years later the faithful 'Herky Bird' is still very much in business.

Hercules the Hero

Of course, the RAF's commitments both in the UK and around the world go far beyond the roles of offensive and defensive aircraft. Although the 'glamour' might be reserved for types such as the Tornado and Harrier, the RAF operates many other vitally important aircraft. One in particular, the ubiquitous Lockheed C-130 Hercules, has become one of the Service's most vital assets, and its tasks continue to grow seemingly week by week. Entering RAF service towards the end of the 1960s, the Hercules first caught the public's attention in the 1970s, when the first famine relief flights were flown to Africa. However, it was the

1982 Falklands conflict which really emphasised the importance of the versatile Hercules, which made a flight to Ascension Island every four hours at the height of the crisis. During the first three weeks of the Falklands conflict some 3.75 million pounds of supplies were moved by the RAF's Hercules force. The Hercules was also a major participant in the Gulf War, and humanitarian flights to various parts of the world continue to this day.

After more than a quarter of a century of operations, it is hardly surprising that the Hercules is now approaching the end of its service life, and aircraft are already beginning

Right: Performing a magnificent formation fly-by, a Hercules C.1P wearing the latest all-grey camouflage leads a C.1K tanker (now retired) and a short-fuselage C.1P flanked by two C.3P 'stretched' variants.

Above: Developed as a result of the Falklands conflict, the C.1K tanker gave the RAF Hercules force a valuable self-supporting tanker capability. Not surprisingly, the handful of Hercules tankers were also regularly used to support other RAF aircraft.

Left: A look into the cargo hold of a Hercules C.1P, illustrating the seating arrangement fitted for troop transport. These seats can all be removed to allow cargo to be carried. Although some sound and heat insulation is visible, the 'Herky Bird's' cargo hold is notoriously noisy.

Below: To mark 25 years of service with the RAF, one aircraft was specially decorated to incorporate the badges of each of the Lyneham Transport Wing (LTW) squadrons.

to be withdrawn from the pool of aircraft based at RAF Lyneham in Wiltshire. But if the late 1990s mark the end of a long and successful career for the Hercules, it is reassuring to know that the new millennium will see the RAF beginning what will hopefully be a long association with a completely new Hercules in the shape of the C-130J, the latest variant being produced by Lockheed Martin. With new engines and digital avionics, the new Hercules (in both short and stretched-fuselage versions) will give the RAF not only a completely new airframe, but one that performs even more impressively that the first-generation model which has served the RAF for so long.

Right: A close-up of a Hercules C.1P from the Lyneham Transport Wing. The grey/green camouflage is now being replaced by a new all-grey scheme.

Right: The RAF's sole Hercules W.2, used for weather reconnaissance duties, is operated by the Meteorological Research Flight based at Boscombe Down.

Maritime Menu

The RAF's maritime assets are also
about to enter a completely new era,
following the completion of a long
study into possible replacements for the
Hawker Siddeley Nimrod anti-submarine
warfare (ASW) and maritime patrol aircraft.
Although design submissions were made for
aircraft such as the Breguet Atlantic and
Lockheed Orion, the RAF opted for a British
Aerospace proposal to refurbish the existing
Nimrod fleet. This might sound like a typical
British compromise, but in reality the 'Nimrod
2000' programme will give the RAF what are,
in effect, completely new aircraft. For
example, some 60 per cent of the airframe
will be built from scratch, including a
completely new wing housing four new-
technology BMW Rolls-Royce BR.710 engines.
The remaining airframe will be refurbished to

produce 'zero-life' components, and the
result will be an all-new aircraft which does
not require the expense of a corresponding
all-new support infrastructure or training
programme. Nimrod 2000 will provide a
variety of improvements upon what was
already a very impressive machine. Range will
be extended to a staggering 15 hours
(equating to a range of over 6,000 nautical
miles), and the search radar system will be
upgraded. The flight deck and cabin synthetic
displays will all be new, and a whole range of
new sensors and defensive systems will be
fitted.

Given that the Soviet submarine threat is
now gone, one could question the need for
such a sophisticated aircraft, but it is impos-
sible to predict future needs, and a truly
capable ASW aircraft cannot be 'invented'

overnight. Purchasing an 'off-the-shelf' design would have saved little when one considers the potential expense of introducing a completely new aircraft type into RAF service. The Nimrod MR.4, as it will almost certainly be designated, will gradually replace the existing MR.2P fleet based at Kinloss in Scotland, achieving operational status in 2003. A total of 21 aircraft will be manufactured, drawn from the current pool of 27 existing airframes. Only three first-generation Nimrods are likely to remain in service, these being the two R.1P and single R.2P aircraft operated by No. 51 Squadron at Waddington in the secretive electronic-intelligence-gathering role.

Below: Complete with 80th anniversary tail markings, a Nimrod MR.2P shows its open weapons-bay doors.

Left: This underside view illustrates the size of the Nimrod's capacious weapons bay, capable of carrying torpedoes, depth charges and SAR equipment.

Right: Seconds before touchdown, a Nimrod MR.2 streaks over the threshold of runway 31 at RAF St Mawgan, Cornwall, where the type entered RAF service in 1970.

Right: Three Nimrods are operated by No. 51 Squadron at Waddington. Assigned to secretive electronic intelligence (Elint) and signals intelligence (Sigint) gathering duties, they have been refitted with in-flight-refuelling equipment, like their maritime counterparts.

Right: The frontal view of a Nimrod MR.2P emphasises the 'double-bubble' fuselage based on the Comet airliner's airframe.

Bottom right: The Nimrod was a direct development of the Comet, the world's first jet airliner, and a type which provided the RAF with a high-speed transport for many years. The last flying example of the Comet was the Defence Research Agency's Canopus, retired in 1997.

Left: Following the withdrawal of No. 2 FTS's Westland/ Aérospatiale Gazelles, basic helicopter training is now conducted by the Defence Helicopter Flying School, equipped with Eurocopter Squirrel HT.1s.

Left: The Westland Wessex advanced helicopter trainers of No. 2 FTS have also been retired, with the Bell Griffin HT.1s of No. 60(R) Squadron assuming their role.

Rotary Roster

elicopter operations also form an increasingly important part of RAF operations, the Service having been involved in this field of activity for as long as the practical helicopter has been in existence. The helicopter has attained a significant status, providing the RAF with medium- and heavy-lift capabilities to countless remote locations around the world. At present the RAF operates three transport support helicopter types, the Westland Wessex, Westland/Aérospatiale Puma and Boeing Vertol Chinook.

The venerable Wessex is now approaching the end of its service life, having been completely withdrawn from the SAR role during 1997. However, it remains active with No. 72 Squadron, based at Aldergrove in support of Army operations in Northern Ireland, and a further five aircraft remain in

service with No. 84 Squadron at Akrotiri in Cyprus.

The Puma, operated by No. 230 Squadron at Aldergrove, No. 33 Squadron at Benson and No. 27(R) Squadron at Odiham (for training on the type), primarily supports the British Army and, like the Wessex, is responsible for carrying equipment and personnel as required, regularly participating in Army exercises in the UK and Germany. For heavy-lift operations the RAF maintains a fleet of Chinook HC.2s with Nos. 7 and 27(R) Squadrons at Odiham, No. 18 Squadron at Laarbruch and No. 78 Squadron at Mount Pleasant on the Falkland Islands. Also assigned to the support of Army operations, the Chinook, like the Puma, will soon be joined by a completely new helicopter in the shape of the Merlin HC.3, currently under development by Westland (European

Right: The Westland/Aérospatiale Puma medium-lift helicopter transport supports Army operations both in the UK and abroad. Heavy-lift operations are undertaken by Chinooks.

Industries). Unlike its predecessors, the Merlin will have an in-flight-refuelling capability and will, of course, incorporate all the latest advances in navigation, communications and self-protection capability. The Merlin's load-carrying capability will place it somewhere between the Puma and Chinook. Although it will effectively replace the Wessex, it is actually an addition to Nato's inventory, as the Wessex has not been declared to Nato for some time.

Training for helicopter operations is concentrated at Shawbury in Shropshire, where the Defence Helicopter Flying School (DHFS) has now been formed. Incorporated into the DHFS is No. 60(R) Squadron, operating a fleet of Eurocopter Squirrel HT.1 helicopters for basic flying training, and larger Bell Griffin HT.1 helicopters for more advanced instruction. A detachment of Griffins is also maintained at Valley for SAR helicopter training, from where students will progress to No. 203(R) Squadron at St Mawgan for conversion on to the Westland Sea King HAR.3, which is now the sole type employed by the RAF on SAR helicopter operations.

Right: A Wessex of No. 60 Squadron, shortly before the unit disbanded. It is now back in business as an advanced helicopter training unit at Shawbury.

Left: Although relatively aged when compared with the latest generation of support helicopters, the Puma is still a very agile performer when necessary, as illustrated by this vertical nose-down manoeuvre.

Right: A No. 78 Squadron Chinook HC.2 at rest on typical Falklands terrain during 1996.

Left: A No. 33 Squadron Puma low over Oxfordshire during a sortie from RAF Benson.

Right: No. 78 Squadron also operates the Sea King for light transport duties and SAR operations.

Above: No. 2 FTS has now said goodbye to the Wessex and disbanded. Helicopter training is now conducted by the Defence Helicopter Flying School, using Squirrels and Griffins.

Left: A Chinook HC.2 in temporary UN colours demonstrates its heavy-lift capability.

Above: A No. 202 Squadron Sea King HAR.3, the RAF's standard SAR helicopter.

Right: The Aérospatiale Gazelle was primarily operated by the RAF as a basic helicopter trainer. However, aircraft operated by No. 2 FTS, were occasionally used for communications duties when required, although two were assigned exclusively to this role with No. 32 Squadron. They have now been replaced by Eurocopter Squirrels.

Postscript

This account has provided merely an overview of current RAF operations, although the captions accompanying the illustrations will serve to demonstrate just how diverse and numerous the RAF's current flying activities are. Although it is much smaller and leaner than ever before, the RAF has more commitments than at almost any other time in its illustrious history. The very fact that the men and women of the RAF continue to provide the UK with what is, without doubt, the best military air arm in the world, testifies to their great skill and continued professionalism. The RAF's 80 years have been filled with fascinating developments, and one can only wonder at the kind of RAF this country might be celebrating in 2018.

Below: A Tornado F.3 of No. 43 Squadron climbs away from Marham, en route for Leuchars, its home base.